Themes to Inspire

1

FOR KS3

Steve Clarke

DYNAMIC LEARNING

HODDER EDUCATION
AN HACHETTE UK COMPANY

Although every effort has been made to ensure that website addresses are correct at time of going to press, Hodder Education cannot be held responsible for the content of any website mentioned in this book. It is sometimes possible to find a relocated web page by typing in the address of the home page for a website in the URL window of your browser.

Hachette UK's policy is to use papers that are natural, renewable and recyclable products and made from wood grown in sustainable forests. The logging and manufacturing processes are expected to conform to the environmental regulations of the country of origin.

Orders: please contact Bookpoint Ltd, 130 Milton Park, Abingdon, Oxon OX14 4SB. Telephone: (44) 01235 827720. Fax: (44) 01235 400454. Lines are open 9.00–5.00, Monday to Saturday, with a 24–hour message answering service. Visit our website at www.hoddereducation.co.uk

© Steve Clarke 2011
First published in 2011 by
Hodder Education,
An Hachette UK Company
338 Euston Road
London NW1 3BH

Impression number   5 4 3 2 1
Year   2015 2014 2013 2012 2011

All rights reserved. Apart from any use permitted under UK copyright law, no part of this publication may be reproduced or transmitted in any form or by any means, electronic or mechanical, including photocopying and recording, or held within any information storage and retrieval system, without permission in writing from the publisher or under licence from the Copyright Licensing Agency Limited. Further details of such licences (for reprographic reproduction) may be obtained from the Copyright Licensing Agency Limited, Saffron House, 6–10 Kirby Street, London EC1N 8TS.

Cover photo: Image of butterfly © Doug Landreth Corbis
Illustrations by *Barking Dog Art, Oxford Designers and Illustrators, Peter Lubach, Richard Duszczak and Tony Randell*
Designed in *Minion Regular* by *The Wooden Ark Ltd (Leeds)*
Printed in Italy

A catalogue record for this title is available from the British Library

ISBN: 978 1444 12205 3

Contents

Section 1

Expressions of faith
- **1.1** How are symbols used in religion? — **4**
- **1.2** How did the religions start? — **8**
- **1.3** What makes a good teacher? — **10**
- **1.4** What do non-Christian religions think about Jesus? — **12**
- **1.5** How do the religions use symbols in art? — **16**
- **1.6** What will you find in a place of worship? — **20**
- **1.7** What will you find in the homes of some religious people? — **24**
- **1.8** How did the religions develop? — **27**

The big assignment — **30**

Section 2

Beliefs and teachings about meaning and purpose
- **2.1** Who am I? — **32**
- **2.2** Where do I belong? — **34**
- **2.3** What is faith? — **36**
- **2.4** What is religion? — **38**
- **2.5** Who or what is God? — **40**
- **2.6** What is life? — **44**
- **2.7** Did the universe have a beginning? — **48**
- **2.8** Will the universe have an end? — **52**

The big assignment — **56**

Section 3

Ethics and values
- **3.1** How do we know right from wrong? — **58**
- **3.2** What makes something good? — **62**
- **3.3** What is the Golden Rule? — **66**
- **3.4** What is a moral dilemma? — **70**
- **3.5** How can you solve a moral dilemma? — **74**
- **3.6** What is love? — **78**
- **3.7** What is justice? — **82**
- **3.8** Why is forgiveness important? — **86**

The big assignment — **90**

Glossary — **92**
Index — **95**
Acknowledgements — **96**

1.1 How are symbols used in religion?

Learning objectives

You will ...
- learn about how symbols are used to express ideas
- understand how to interpret symbols
- design symbols to represent ideas
- link symbols with religious beliefs
- interpret different religious symbols.

Some ideas or feelings are very complicated and cannot be explained easily in words. One way to do it is to use **symbols**.

If you wanted to represent **Strength, leadership, wisdom, power, grace, and elegance** what symbols would you use?

Civilisations throughout history have used the eagle as a symbol of these qualities:
- The eagle was a symbol of the Roman Empire.
- Native Americans wear eagle feathers as symbols.
- The eagle features on the seal of the President of the United States of America.
- St John, one of the gospel writers in the Christian Bible, is often represented as an eagle.

Here are some other popular symbols:

Scales are used as a symbol of justice, fairness and the law. A judge has to 'weigh up' evidence in order to make a fair decision.

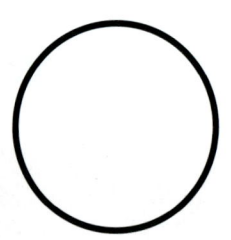

A circle can represent eternity, because it has no beginning and no end.

A heart symbolises love, because it used to be thought that human emotions came from the heart. It is often red to show passion, which can make the heart beat faster and pump more blood.

Sometimes the human body is used to make symbols:

Picture 1.

Picture 2.

Picture 3.

Picture 4.

Knowledge check

Look at pictures 1–4. What do the body positions mean?

Religious symbols

Symbols are used as simple ways to express complex ideas. Here is a diagrammatic symbol of the **Trinity** – the Christian idea of God. It shows the three aspects of the one God – Father, Son and Holy Spirit – and it shows the relationships between them.

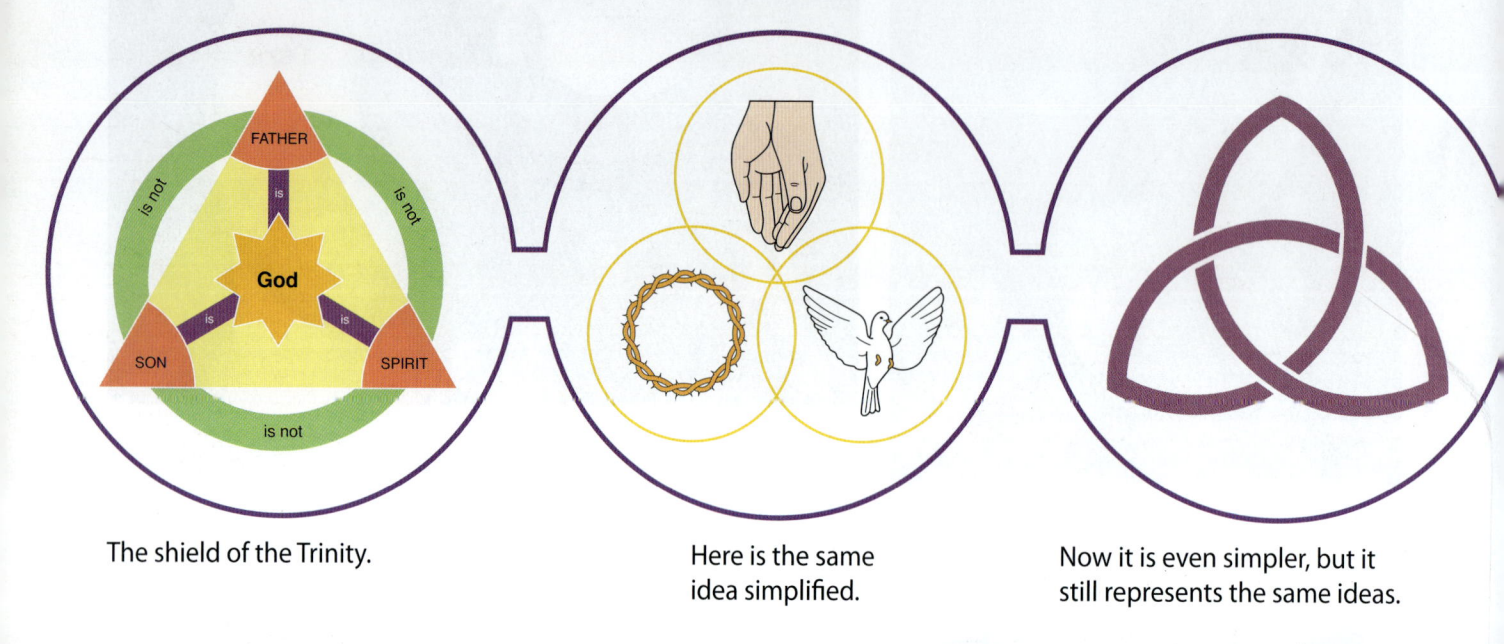

The shield of the Trinity.

Here is the same idea simplified.

Now it is even simpler, but it still represents the same ideas.

Activity A

1. Design your own symbols for at least four of the following ideas:

   respect   goodness   sorrow
   courage   beauty   boredom   fear   anger
   wisdom   intelligence   failure
   honesty   pride   loyalty   freedom
   sympathy   forgiveness   life

2. Explain to a partner why you have chosen them.

3. Share your symbols with three or four other people. Can they guess what the symbols mean?

4. Make your symbols into a poster and create a classroom display.

Religions have symbols that represent some of their most important beliefs:

Activity B

1. Find out which religions are represented by the symbols shown above.
2. What beliefs do they symbolise?

Activity C

1. Do some research to produce a booklet explaining how symbols are used in one religion of your choosing.
2. Find out about the way symbols are used in religious dress, body positions in worship, architecture, festivals, stories and works of art. You should not only describe the symbols, but also explain what beliefs or ideas they express.

Activity D

1. Find out about how Jesus is represented by Christians in different countries and at different points in history.
2. Produce an illustrated guide showing how the different representations reflect the culture or time period they come from, and how beliefs about Jesus have different emphases in different cultures and time periods.

1.2 How did the religions start?

Learning objectives

You will ...
- find out about when and where religions started
- understand why religious people value early religious teachers
- understand what it means to follow a faith.

None of the men mentioned in the map below intended to start a new religion. In most cases, they felt the experience of encountering God. An experience like this is called a **revelation**. They were able to inspire other people to accept what they had learnt.

A map showing when and where the religions started.

Knowledge check

1. Where did Hinduism develop?
2. From which religious traditions did Buddhism emerge?
3. Who can Judaism be traced to?
4. In which century did Jesus live?
5. Who was the greatest messenger of Islam?
6. Which religion tries to unite Hinduism and Islam?
7. What is a revelation?

❶ Christianity started about 2,000 years ago when followers of Jesus (who was himself Jewish) developed a new understanding of God.

❷ Islam began in 610CE when Muhammad, believed by Muslims to be the greatest of God's prophets, received his first message from God.

❸ Sikhism is the newest of the world's major faiths. Nanak, a Hindu, believed that God was too big to be tied to one religion. At the beginning of the sixteenth century, he tried to bring Hindus and Muslims together to share the same faith.

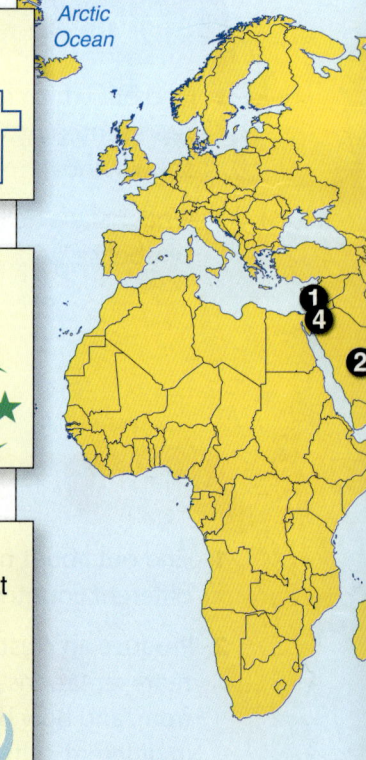

Activity A

1. Make a timeline of the beginnings of the main religions. You could make a wall display.
2. Try to find out about some other religions, and add them to your timeline. Use pictures or symbols to illustrate it.

Activity B

Plan an interview with a believer (from any faith) about the person who inspired their religion.

1. What questions would you ask to find out why that person is so important?
2. Think about why people followed him or what he had to say, why people are still inspired today, and what difference he has made to their lives.
3. What answers would you expect?

Activity C

1. The word *follow* means a number of things. Write down all the meanings you know. Then talk to a partner and see if there are any you have missed.
2. When a person says that they follow a religion, what do they mean? Use the definitions you have identified, and choose the most appropriate. Why have you chosen them? Can you give some examples?

Activity D

'Faith is the great cop-out, a great excuse to avoid the need to think.'
(Richard Dawkins, untitled lecture, Edinburgh Science Festival 1992)

1. How far do you think following the teachings of a religious leader is avoiding the need to think for oneself?
2. Do you think that religious and spiritual truths can be passed from one person to another?

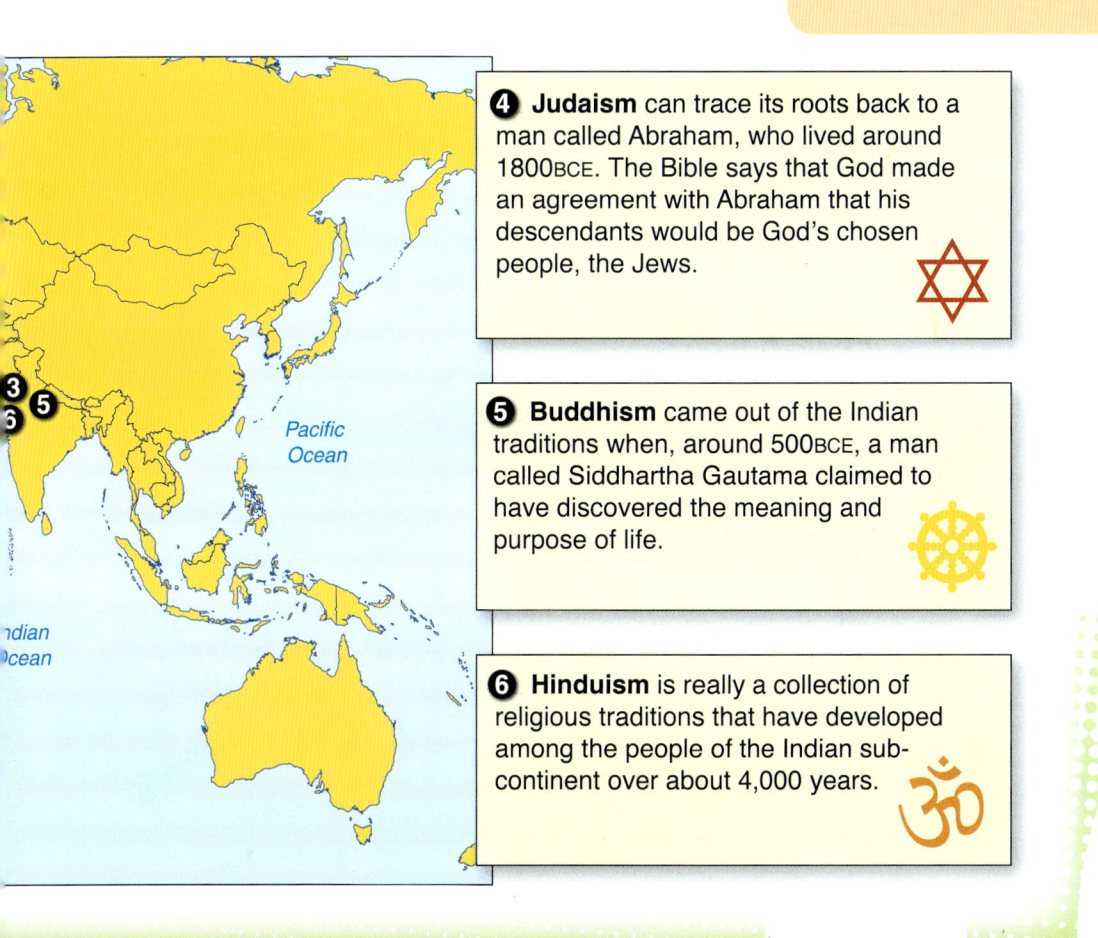

---

❹ **Judaism** can trace its roots back to a man called Abraham, who lived around 1800 BCE. The Bible says that God made an agreement with Abraham that his descendants would be God's chosen people, the Jews.

❺ **Buddhism** came out of the Indian traditions when, around 500 BCE, a man called Siddhartha Gautama claimed to have discovered the meaning and purpose of life.

❻ **Hinduism** is really a collection of religious traditions that have developed among the people of the Indian sub-continent over about 4,000 years.

1.3 What makes a good teacher?

Learning objectives

You will ...
- learn about what different people think makes a good teacher
- consider your views on what makes a good teacher
- analyse how a good teacher may put his or her skills into practice.

The people we looked at in the previous chapter felt that they had a new understanding of God, or of life and the way that people should live it. They felt inspired to teach other people what they had learnt.

When some Year 8 pupils were asked, '*What makes a good teacher?*' they came up with the following list:

A good teacher ...

- ... tells you how you're doing.
- ... is generous.
- ... makes you feel clever.
- ... tells the truth.
- ... stands up for you.
- ... listens to you.
- ... cares for your opinion.
- ... makes allowances.
- ... helps you when you're stuck.
- ... encourages you.
- ... is kind.
- ... has faith in you.
- ... likes teaching their subject.
- ... treats people equally.
- ... is forgiving.
- ... takes time to explain things.
- ... doesn't give up on you.
- ... keeps confidences.
- ... allows you to have your say.

Activity A

1. What are *your* top ten characteristics of a good teacher? Think about the good teachers you know. How do they make learning easy? How do they motivate you?
2. Now pick your top three characteristics.
3. Once you have written out your list, draw symbols for your top three.

Zen Buddhist stories

Story 1

A new student approached a Zen Buddhist master and asked how he should prepare himself for his training.

'Think of me as a bell,' the master explained. 'Give me a soft tap, and you will get a tiny ping. Strike hard, and you'll receive a loud, resounding peal.'

Story 2

One evening as Zen Master Shichiri Kojun was reciting sutras (Buddhist writings) a thief with a sharp sword entered, demanding either money or his life.

Shichiri told him, 'Do not disturb me. You can find the money in that drawer.' Then he went back to his recitation.

A little while afterwards he stopped and called to the thief, 'Don't take it all. I need some for tomorrow.'

The intruder gathered up most of the money and started to leave. 'Thank a person when you receive a gift,' Shichiri added. The man thanked him and made off.

A few days afterwards the thief was caught and confessed that he had robbed a lot of people. When Shichiri was called as a witness he said, 'This man is no thief, at least as far as I am concerned. I gave him money and he thanked me for it.'

After he had finished his prison term, the man went to Shichiri and became his disciple.

Activity B

1. What does Story 1 mean? What does it say about teaching and learning? Write your answer in one sentence.
2. Now ask other members of your class what they think. How many different answers are there? Is there a right answer to the questions? Are there any you disagree with? Why?

Activity C

1. Which of the qualities of a good teacher does Shichiri show in Story 2? Explain your answer.
2. Write a story of your own to show how a teacher or coach can use his or her qualities.

Activity D

1. Use books and the Internet to conduct some research into religious teachers from the same faith. Which of the qualities of a good teacher does each of them demonstrate?
2. Use examples from their lives to support your views.

1.4 What do non-Christian religions think about Jesus?

Learning objectives

You will …
- understand that Jesus does not belong to Christianity alone
- find out what Hindus and Muslims believe about Jesus
- research different views about Jesus within Judaism
- think about Jesus as a Buddhist might.

Jesus is, of course, of central importance to Christians. For Christians, he is one person of the Trinity. He is both God and a human being.

But Jesus is important to other faiths for different reasons. For them, Jesus does not 'belong' to Christianity.

Hinduism

Jesus is known by Hindus as Ishu. For some, he was a saint who performed great miracles and taught wonderful things about how people should live.

For others Jesus was a **sadhu**, a wandering holy man, dedicated to escaping the cycle of birth and death to become one with God.

Still others say that Jesus was an **avatar**, or physical appearance, of God on earth.

Knowledge check

Look at pages 12–13.

1. According to Christians, is Jesus God or a human being?
2. By what name is Jesus known in the Hindu traditions?
3. What is a sadhu?
4. What is an avatar?
5. By what name is Jesus known to Muslims?
6. Who do Muslims believe Jesus was?

Islam

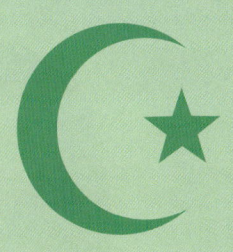

In Islam, Jesus, or Isa as he is called in the Qur'an, was one of the thousands of **prophets** through whom God has spoken to human beings.

Muslims do not believe that Jesus was put to death by being nailed to a cross; the Qur'an says that he rose alive to be with **Allah**.

They also believe that he will come again just before the end of the world.

Isa, as a prophet of Allah, being helped by angels.

Images of Jesus from different religious traditions.

Activity A

1. Look carefully at the three pictures of Jesus. Each comes from a different religious tradition. Can you work out which?
2. Give reasons for your answer.

Activity B

1. Get into groups of three. Read the story of the birth of Isa from the Qur'an (Maryam 19:16–36), and the two stories of Jesus' birth in the Bible (Matthew 1:18–2:12 and Luke 2:1–20).
   - One person from the group should record all the things from the account in the *Qur'an* that are different from the other two.
   - One person from the group should record all the things from *Matthew's* account in the Bible that are different from the other two.
   - One person from the group should record all the things from *Luke's* account in the Bible that are different from the other two.
2. Explain to the others in your group what each writer is trying to say about Jesus.

Activity C

1. Jesus was born in a Jewish country and was a Jew. Find out about different views Jews have today about Jesus and who he was.
2. Present your findings in question-and-answer format.

A Buddhist Story

One of Master Gasan's monks visited the university in Tokyo. When he returned, he asked the master if he had ever read the Christian Bible.

'No,' Gasan replied, 'please read some of it to me.'

The monk opened the Bible at the Sermon on the Mount in Matthew's Gospel and began reading. After reading Christ's words about the lilies in the field, he paused. Master Gasan was silent for a long time.

'Yes,' he finally said, 'whoever uttered these words is an **enlightened being**. What you have read to me is the essence of everything I have been trying to teach you here!'

Activity D

1. Read A Buddhist Story.
2. Now read the passage from the Bible referred to in the story in Matthew 6:24–34.
3. Conduct some research to find answers to the following questions:
   a. What is an enlightened being?
   b. What does **dukkha** mean to a Buddhist?
   c. How do Buddhists believe people can overcome dukkha?
4. Now read the final paragraph again. What does Master Gasan mean when he says this?

1.5 How do the religions use symbols in art?

Learning objectives

You will …
- discover the meanings of symbols in religious art
- interpret religious symbols in art
- use symbols in representing people
- compare symbols of different religions.

It is said that every picture tells a story. In religious art, pictures often contain symbols to help you read the story. But you have to know what the symbols mean in order to be able to 'read' the pictures properly.

Buddhism

The dot on the Buddha's forehead represents the Eye of Wisdom, showing his deep understanding of life.

The Buddha has long ear lobes, showing he comes from a wealthy family. Gold earrings have stretched his ear lobes.

The Buddha's right hand is held up and facing out, a symbol of fearlessness.

The Buddha's head is surrounded by a halo, showing his advanced spiritual nature.

The Buddha's left hand is pointing downwards and facing out, a symbol of generosity.

The Buddha sits with his legs crossed. He is concentrating.

The Buddha.

Knowledge check

Look at all the images on pages 16–19.
1. What is a halo?
2. What does the colour white symbolise in Christian art?
3. Why are some men shown wearing beards in religious art?
4. How is the Buddha shown to be fearless in art?
5. Look at the picture of Ganesha on page 18. What sort of head does he have?
6. Can you see a mouse at Ganesha's feet? See if you can find out why it is there.

16

Christianity

No one knows what Jesus looked like, but he is shown with a beard – a symbol of a religious teacher.

The first letter of the Greek word, Christos (Christ) is X. Jesus crosses his fingers to represent this letter.

Jesus' other two fingers show that he was both God and a man.

The Sacred Heart represents God's love. It is wrapped by a crown of thorns, as was Jesus' head before he died. The cross on which he died is shown above it. Light comes from the Heart to show that it comes from God.

A ring of light – a halo – around Jesus' head shows that he has a holy mission.

Jesus puts the middle three fingers of his left hand together to represent the Trinity.

Red is a symbol of the power of God.

White is a symbol of purity.

Gold is a symbol of **divinity**.

A popular representation of Jesus.

Mary, the mother of Jesus, has an **aureole**: light comes from her showing that she is favoured by God.

White is a symbol of purity.

Mary's hands are held together in prayer.

Blue is a symbol of heaven.

Mary is on a cloud held by angels, a symbol of heaven and respect.

A popular representation of Mary.

Hinduism

Ganesha has a big head: he is clever.

Ganesha has big ears: he hears people's prayers.

Ganesha has a halo: he is a representation of God.

With the rope in his left hand Ganesha can pull people up to their full potential.

The axe shows that Ganesha has cut ties with worldly things.

Ganesha's tusks represent good and evil. He has broken the evil one off.

Ganesha has a bowl of sweets: good **karma**.

A large stomach is a sign of contentment.

Ganesha holds a right hand upwards and facing out, giving his blessing.

Ganesha.

Activity A

1. Think of someone you admire. Try to represent that person using some of the symbols you have learnt about on pages 16–19.
2. What colours will you use, and why? What positions will you put the hands or the body into, and what will the positions show? What other symbols will you use?

Activity B

1. In some branches of Christianity, especially the Orthodox and Roman Catholic Churches, people use pictures called *icons* to help them understand their faith better. Find out about the symbols used in making icons and how icons are used to help people worship.
2. Present your findings in the form of a brochure.

Sikhism

Guru Nanak has a halo and an aureole.

Guru Nanak has a beard – a symbol of a religious teacher.

Nanak's friends are taking care of him, showing that he is worthy of respect.

Guru Nanak.

The gold of Nanak's robe is a symbol of strength and importance.

Nanak sits on a mat, separating him from the earth.

Activity C

1. Colours are used a lot as symbols in art and elsewhere. Find out about the different things that colours symbolise in different religions.
2. Make a colour chart, and show within each colour what it represents.
3. Sometimes different colours can be interpreted in different ways, depending upon the culture. Can you find any examples of this?

Activity D

1. Produce an illustrated guide to show how symbols are used in religious art. You could organise your guide in sections to include colours, hand gestures, halos and aureoles, and clothes.
2. Try to find examples from a range of religions.

1.6 What will you find in a place of worship?

Learning objectives

You will …
- find out about the features that you might see in a place of worship
- understand why these features are important to worshippers
- compare places of worship between and within religions.

Most branches of most religions have buildings that are used specifically for people to worship in. Each of these buildings is unique. Yet within each religion there are common features – objects you would expect to find. There are some features that you may find in buildings from a variety of religions. You can see some of them on pages 20–23.

In some places of worship, worshippers face in a particular direction. In **mosques**, Muslims face the city of Makkah, where the Ka'aba, the House of God, is situated. The direction of the Ka'aba is indicated by an alcove in a wall, called the **mihrab**.

Some places of worship have a focal point of worship. This picture of a **synagogue** shows the **ark**, which Jews face when worshipping. It is a cupboard that contains holy writings on scrolls. Jews do not worship the scrolls, but they form a point of concentration.

Knowledge check

1. Which place of worship contains a mihrab?
2. What does an ark contain?
3. Where do Sikhs sit when they worship in a gurdwara?
4. Where might you find Stations of the Cross?
5. What do some worshippers burn to create a spiritual atmosphere in a place of worship?
6. Why do people make offerings in places of worship?

It is not unusual for men and women to be separated in some places of worship. In Sikh gurdwaras, men and women sit separately on the floor.

Many places of worship have pictures or statues to help people worship. Some churches have fourteen or fifteen pictures of the last hours of Jesus' life around the walls. They are called Stations of the Cross.

It is common to fill places of worship with rich scents to give them a spiritual atmosphere to help worship. At this Buddhist temple in Hong Kong, incense is being burnt.

In many places of worship, offerings, including food, flowers and water are made, showing respect for God or an object of worship. In this Hindu temple, offerings are being made at a wedding.

21

Often, during worship, a religious leader will give a talk to explain aspects of the faith to worshippers. Some places of worship have a special place for the speaker to stand. In a mosque, it looks like a staircase, and is called a **minbar**.

Many places of worship have a special stand to hold a holy book while it is being read to the worshippers. This **lectern** is in a church.

Music often plays a part in worship, and singing is accompanied by musical instruments. In this **gurdwara**, musicians are playing harmoniums and tabla drums.

Knowledge check

1. What is a minbar?
2. What is a lectern used for?
3. Which instruments are used to create music in a gurdwara?

Activity A

1. Find out about places of worship from two different religions.
2. Draw floor plans (i.e. overhead maps) of them, labelling the important features.

Activity B

1. Find out about places of worship from two different religions.
2. Produce a visitors' guide for each, describing what the visitor will see, and explaining why these features are there, and how they are used. You should illustrate your guides using diagrams and pictures.

This is Brick Lane Mosque in the East End of London. It started out as a chapel for French Protestant Christians in the middle of the eighteenth century. At the beginning of the nineteenth century it became a Methodist chapel, and later a synagogue. In the 1970s the area became populated by Muslims from Bangladesh, and the building was converted into a mosque.

Activity C

1. Find out about two places of worship from different branches of the same faith. Draw floor plans of each, labelling the important features.
2. Then write an article to explain why there are differences in the two buildings.

Activity D

1. Design one building that could be used for worship by different religions.
2. You will need to describe the features that most religions would require, and how they could be adapted to fit specific requirements.

1.7 What will you find in the homes of some religious people?

Learning objectives

You will …
- find out about the objects and artefacts that you might see in the homes of religious people
- understand why these objects are important to individuals and families
- understand how these objects are used within the home
- consider the impact of belonging to a religious family.

A place of learning

The homes of religious families are the most important places for passing on beliefs, traditions and practices from generation to generation. Children are able to learn from the examples their parents set. The home itself may contain objects and artefacts that are used as reminders of aspects of the faith, or for prayer and worship.

The photo on the right shows a **mezuzah**. This is a piece of parchment on which is written a short prayer. It is kept in a decorative case and hung on the doorpost of a person's or family's home. It is used by Jews as a reminder of God's presence in the home, and as a sign of welcome to visitors. Jews will touch it as they enter the house, and kiss the fingers that touched it. This is a symbol of love for God and respect for his laws.

A mezuzah.

Knowledge check

1 What is a mezuzah?
2 Which religious group might use a mezuzah?

24

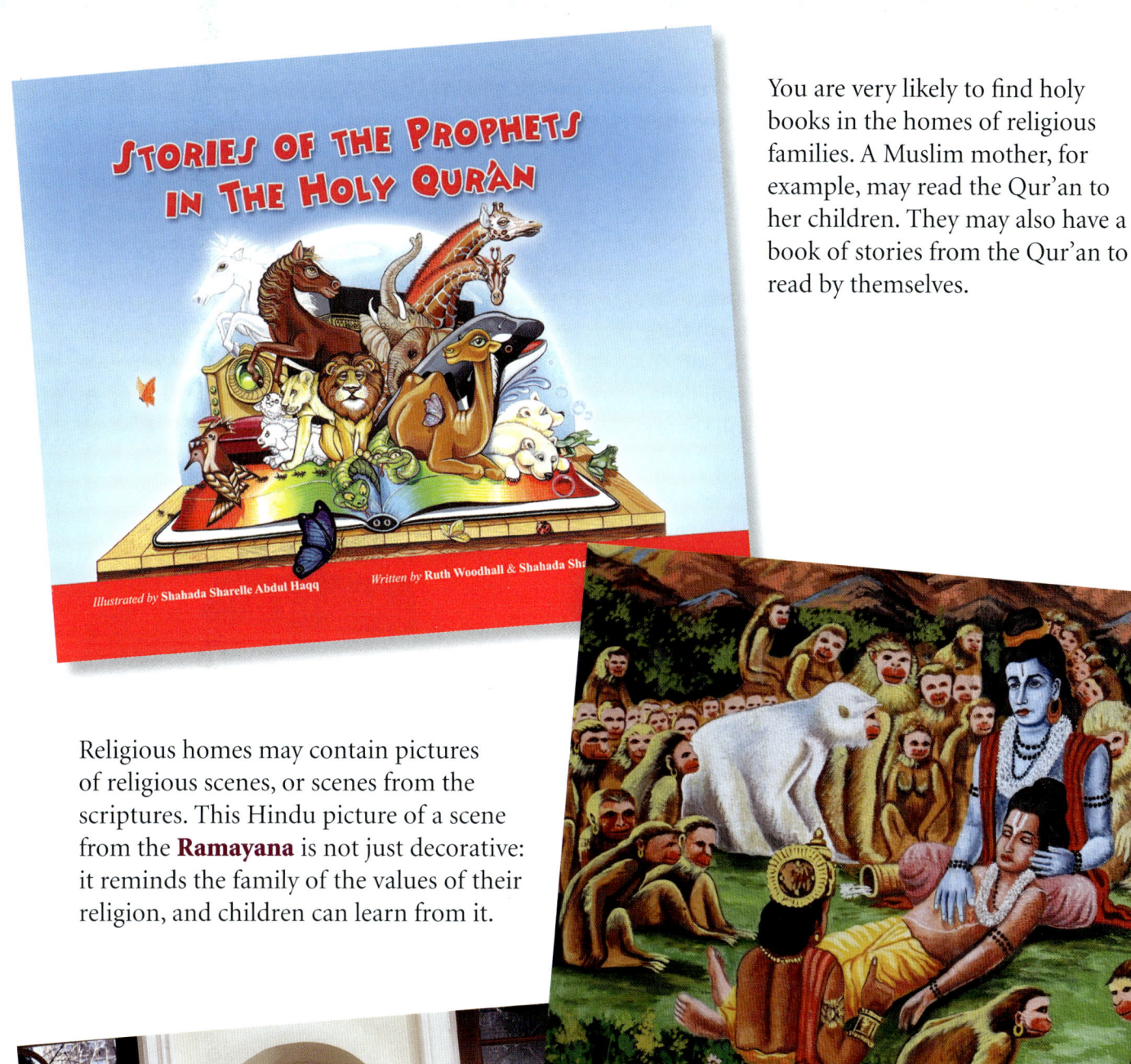

You are very likely to find holy books in the homes of religious families. A Muslim mother, for example, may read the Qur'an to her children. They may also have a book of stories from the Qur'an to read by themselves.

Religious homes may contain pictures of religious scenes, or scenes from the scriptures. This Hindu picture of a scene from the **Ramayana** is not just decorative: it reminds the family of the values of their religion, and children can learn from it.

Some homes may contain a **shrine**, an object or focus for worship. This is a shrine in a Buddhist home. The family may worship together in front of this, or individuals may pray before it when they want to.

There may be religious symbols on the walls of some homes. These act as reminders for the family and their visitors of the values that are held in the home. Some Christian homes have a **crucifix** or cross on the wall to remind them of the importance of Jesus' death.

When families celebrate religious festivals together, or take part in other ceremonies in the home, there will be special objects. At the start of **Shabbat**, for example, a Jewish mother will light candles with her daughter. The family will share a special meal afterwards.

Knowledge check

1 How are religious pictures important in some homes?
2 What happens at a shrine?
3 How does Shabbat start in Jewish households?

Activity A

1 Write an imaginary interview with a person of your age from a religious household.
2 Use questions and answers to find out how objects in the home remind them of their religious beliefs and values.

Activity B

Write a FAQ (Frequently Asked Questions) page for a website to explain the impact that religious objects in the home has on a family.

Activity C

1 What do you think are the challenges or difficulties for a young person coming from a home where religious ideas and values are taught?
2 What do you think the benefits are?
3 Write an article on this for a school newspaper.

Activity D

1 Do you think that children should be brought up to accept religious beliefs? Or should they be left to make up their own minds?
2 What about rules of behaviour? Should children be taught about what is right and wrong, or should they be left to make up their own minds?
3 For each question above give your opinion and back it up by giving as many reasons as you can. Then give as many reasons as you can why some people might disagree with you.

1.8 How did the religions develop?

Learning objectives

You will ...
- find out about how religions spread, grew and divided
- investigate the different branches of a religion
- understand the reasons for divisions within a religion
- understand why people of the same faith have different views about moral issues.

All of the major religions changed in the centuries that followed their beginnings. The changes took three main forms:

1. They spread from the places they started.
2. The numbers of followers increased.
3. They split into different groups.

How did the religions spread?

Some religious followers were **persecuted** and moved to other lands.

For example:

JUDAISM — Two thousand years ago, the Jewish people in Palestine were ruled by the Romans. The Jews tried to fight against the Romans, so the Romans destroyed their capital, Jerusalem, and scattered them to different parts of the Roman Empire.

Some religions sent **missionaries** to other countries to teach people about their faith.

For example:

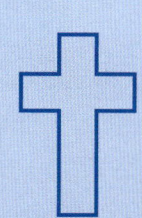

CHRISTIANITY — Jesus told his closest followers that they should teach other people the things that he had taught them. After Jesus' death, his followers travelled far and wide teaching. Many people became **converts** to Christianity.

Knowledge check

1. What is persecution?
2. Who told the first Christians that they should spread Jesus' teachings?

How did their numbers increase?

Trade routes were established connecting people from different parts of the world.
For example:

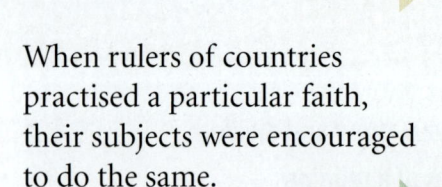

BUDDHISM Buddhist merchants travelled from India to the Far East to buy and sell goods. People they met along the way were impressed by their ideas, and started to practise Buddhism themselves.

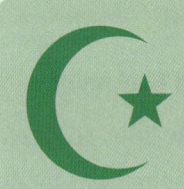

When rulers of countries practised a particular faith, their subjects were encouraged to do the same.
For example:

ISLAM By 631 CE Muhammad was recognised in Arabia as the prophet of God. He extended his leadership over other Arab nations. The people felt secure, believing that a powerful God was protecting them.

Why did the religions split?

People disagreed about **doctrine**.
For example:

BUDDHISM About 150 years after the **Buddha**'s death, his followers disagreed about how strictly his teaching should be followed. They divided into two groups: the Theravada and the Mahayana.

People disagreed about leadership.
For example:

CHRISTIANITY Early Christians were led by one man, the Pope. About 1,000 years after Jesus' death, some Christian groups did not accept the Pope's leadership. They joined together to become the Eastern Orthodox Church. Those who accepted the authority of the Pope remained as the Catholic Church.

Religions adapted to the cultures they moved into.
For example:

JUDAISM After the Romans forced them to leave Palestine, Jews spread throughout Europe. Some settled in Central and Eastern Europe. This group and their descendants are called Ashkenazi Jews. Other Jews settled in Spain, Portugal and North Africa. These are Sephardic Jews.

Knowledge check

1. Name one religion that spread through trade.
2. How did Islam bring strength to the Arab peoples?
3. What are the two main Buddhist groups?
4. Who is the head of the Catholic Church?
5. Where do Ashkenazi Jews originally come from?

The following activities are research activities that involve teamwork. In your groups, you will need to decide how you will present your findings. You could produce a poster, a fact book, an electronic presentation, a display – the choice is yours, so use your imagination.

Activity A

Work in pairs. One person is to investigate Hinayana (which is another name for Theravada) Buddhism; the other, Mahayana Buddhism.

1 Each of you should find out:
   a What the name means.
   b Why it has that name.
   c Three distinctive facts about it.
   d How many people practise that form of Buddhism in the world today.

2 Alternatively, you could investigate Roman Catholic and Eastern Orthodox Christianity, or Sunni and Shi'a Islam.

Activity B

Work in groups of four. Choose one of the following religions:

Buddhism   Christianity   Islam

1 Two of you should investigate how the religion grew. You will need to find out about missionaries setting out to convert people; how new forms of communication between people made it easier; how leaders and rulers helped.

2 Two of you should investigate splits in the religion. You will need to find out about disagreements about doctrine; disagreements about leadership; how religions adapted and changed in different cultural settings.

Activity C

Work in threes. Choose one of the following religions and the branches within it:

Buddhism: Theravada, Mahayana, Vajrayana
Christianity: Orthodox, Roman Catholic, Protestant
Judaism: Orthodox, Conservative, Reform

1 Each person should investigate distinctive features of one of the branches within their chosen religion. For each branch of the religion, find out about:
   - distinctive beliefs and teachings
   - particular individuals or special stories
   - rules about how to live
   - ways of worshipping
   - special clothes, food, buildings and books
   - groups within the branch
   - special feelings and emotions.

2 Compare the results of your research.

Activity D

Work in pairs. Choose one of the following religions:

Christianity   Islam   Judaism

1 Together, investigate different beliefs and attitudes that followers of that religion have about one or more of the following issues:

Abortion   Capital punishment
War   Homosexuality

2 Find out about:
   - the range of different views and beliefs
   - why there is a range of views
   - whether different views are associated with different branches within the religion
   - whether different beliefs are influenced by different countries in which the religion is practised
   - how people put their beliefs into practice in their lives
   - how people with strong views about an issue feel about people with different views within the same religion.

The big assignment

Task

To produce a multimedia guide to a local place of worship.

Objectives

- To research the history, purposes, architecture, artefacts and impacts of a local place of worship.
- To use evidence from religious leaders and/or worshippers to inform your findings.

Outcome

To produce an information pack that could be used by a local place of worship to give information to visitors about what it is and what it does.

You should include information about:

- the history of the place
- what the worshippers do to help other people in the community and the world
- other uses for the building
- the worshippers
- symbols
- services and celebrations
- how the person who inspired the religion is remembered
- the use of art
- some of the feelings people have when they are in a place of worship

Guidance

1. Work in groups of six or seven people. Each person should be given a specific job to do, and the rest of the group should support them in doing it.

2. Suggested jobs:
   a. Asking the leader of a local place of worship to help you with the Big Assignment.
   b. Writing questions to ask the leader of the place of worship.
   c. Asking the questions and writing up the answers.
   d. Filming the interview.
   e. Filming the place of worship (if you are allowed to).
   f. Photographing the objects/artefacts (if you are allowed to).
   g. Writing up descriptions of the building and the objects inside it.
   h. Drawing diagrams and plans to illustrate your descriptions.
   i. Writing up explanations of why the objects are there and how they are used.

3. As a group, go through the evidence, i.e. the outcomes of each job, and for each one decide what needs to be done to finish it.

4. Remember to include instructions for visitors about how they should behave in a place of worship (and why), and how they should treat the artefacts (and why).

5. Your completed information pack should contain your findings in a variety of media: film, photographs, plans, diagrams, writings.

6. Present your information pack to the leader of the place of worship, and ask for feedback.

Assessment

You will be assessed on:
- ✓ how well you use specialist vocabulary
- ✓ your ability to explain the importance of religious objects for worshippers
- ✓ your ability to explain how people should behave in a place of worship, and why.

2.1 Who am I?

Learning objectives

You will …
- explore different views about what a person is
- think about the things that make each person unique
- express a supported view of what makes a human being.

It's easy to describe what a person looks like, even what a person is made of. But that doesn't explain everything about a human being.

Humans can **think**, **plan**, be **afraid**, be **creative**, **remember**, fall in **love**.

So – what is a person? There are two possible answers.

Dualism

1. The first view is called **dualism**, meaning *having two parts*.

A person is a body and something else: a mind or a soul. The soul is separate from the body. The body is a physical thing that you can touch. But thoughts and feelings are not physical, so the soul cannot be physical.

Knowledge check

1. Write a list of things that a human being can do that other physical objects cannot do.
2. What does a dualist believe about what makes up a human being?
3. What does the word dualism mean?
4. What does a physicalist believe?

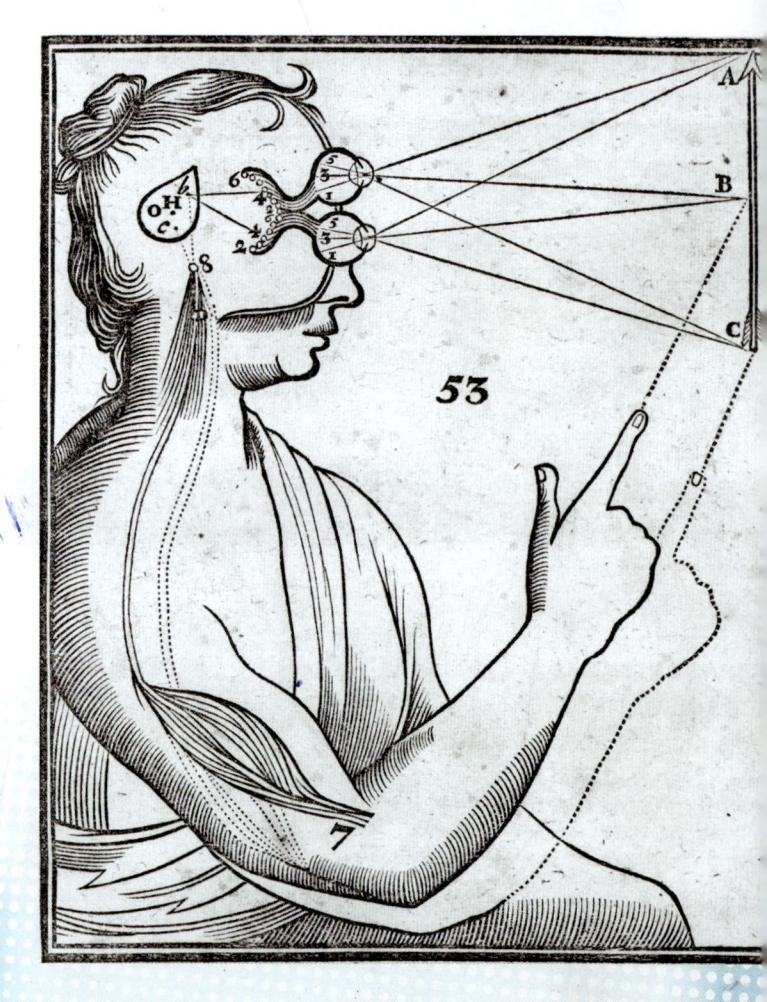

René Descartes was a French **philosopher** who lived in the seventeenth century. He was a dualist, and he made this engraving to show how feeling is transferred to the physical brain, and from there to the non-physical mind.

Physicalism

2 The second view is called **physicalism**. It says that a person is entirely physical.

A person is just a body: a body that can plan, think, communicate and feel things. These abilities are what make a human body a person. According to this view, the mind is part of, and not separate from, the body.

If you have a computer, you know that your computer can play music, remember things, show movies, play games. These abilities are not separate from the computer, they are part of it. In the same way, the mind is part of, and not separate from, the body.

This question, 'Who am I?' is hugely important to the study of religion, because most religious people are dualists, believing that the mind or soul is the essential part of a person.

Is a human being like a computer, programmed to think, communicate and feel things?

Activity A

Write a description of the person sitting next to you *without describing any of their physical features*.

Activity B

1 Each person is unique: there is only one you, and no one else is like you. Draw a poster to represent you.

2 To do this, draw a picture of yourself in the middle of a page, and surround it with descriptions and pictures of the things that are special to you. You could include your favourite music, your favourite foods, clothes, members of your family, friends, pets, people you admire, and anything that might play a part in making you who you are.

Activity C

1 Compare the dualist view of a person with the physicalist view.

2 What is similar? What is different?

Activity D

1 Are you a dualist or a physicalist? Or do you have a different view of what makes a human being?

2 Give reasons for your answer.

2.2 Where do I belong?

Learning objectives

You will …
- learn about the link between personal and social identity
- identify groups that contribute to your personal identity
- evaluate the strength of the family in creating a sense of belonging.

Personal and social identity

Who you are (your **personal identity**) is influenced by the groups you belong to (your **social identity**). Our membership of different groups tells others about the kinds of people, beliefs and values that we want to be associated with, and, in the end, the kinds of people we are.

Here are some of the groups that people belong to that give them a sense of personal identity.

Family The family teaches people what they need to know to live as human beings.

Nationality British people share values, rules and customs with other Britons.

Teams People who support sports teams feel a strong sense of loyalty to the team and to each other.

Friendship This includes school friends, friends outside school, and friends people meet online.

Work Where someone works or goes to school says a lot about what people might think of them.

Age groups People feel comfortable with others of a similar age.

Religion It is thought that the word *religion* comes from the Latin word *ligare*, which means *to bind together*. People of the same religion share beliefs about God, life and death, and also have similar ideas about what is right and wrong. They celebrate together, and support each other when times are difficult. Together religious people welcome the birth of a baby into the world, and commemorate the life of a member who has died. Religions have ceremonies to mark the formation of a new family when two people get married.

Knowledge check

1. What is the difference between personal identity and social identity?
2. Name three groups that contribute to a person's social identity.
3. Explain how these groups contribute to social identity.

Activity A

1. Which parts of your identity are fixed?
2. Which parts of your identity are flexible and can be changed?

Activity B

1. Look back at Activity B on page 33 in which you were asked to draw your personal identity in the form of a poster.
2. Now draw an identity web. You can use your poster as a starting point. Your identity web might look something like this:

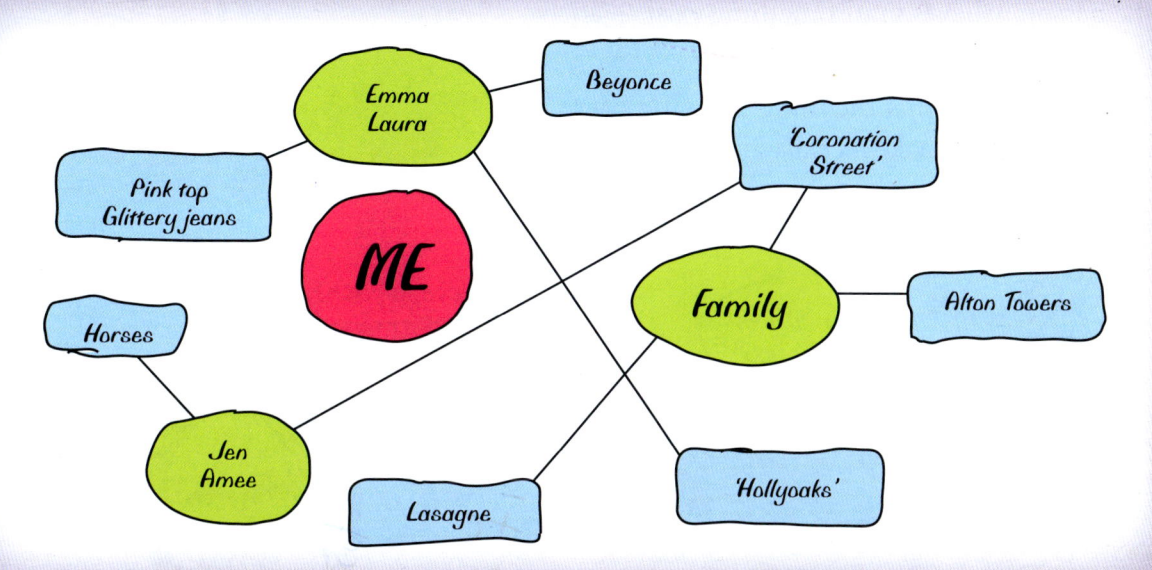

[Identity web diagram with "ME" at centre, connected to: Emma Laura, Beyonce, 'Coronation Street', Pink top Glittery jeans, Family, Alton Towers, Horses, Jen Amee, Lasagne, 'Hollyoaks']

In this web, special things have been put into boxes, and groups into circles. The boxes and circles have been connected by lines to show where they are linked. Your identity web will be much more intricate than this, and may include pictures and symbols.

Activity C

1. What sorts of things give Britain and the British their identity?
2. Remember that Britain contains a wide variety of different groups. What sorts of things make people feel they belong in Britain?
3. In pairs, write a list of ten things that make Britain what it is.
4. Now, use these ideas to make a survey to find out other people's views.

Activity D

'The family is the most important part of a person's identity.'

1. Discuss this statement with a partner. Think of three reasons why some people may agree with it.
2. Then think of three reasons why others may disagree.

2.3 What is faith?

Learning objectives

You will ...
- learn about different meanings of *belief in*
- learn about what *faith* means for religious people
- think of how religious faith could be put into action.

What do people mean when they say 'I believe in ...'?

In these examples on the right, *belief in* means two things:

1. The person believes that something exists – aliens, ghosts, Father Christmas, fairies.
2. There is no proof that the thing exists, or not enough proof to make its existence a fact.

I believe in aliens.

I believe in ghosts.

I believe in Father Christmas.

I believe in fairies.

"You can do it! I believe in you!"

In the example on the left, the tennis player's mum is not saying to her son 'I believe you exist.'! She is talking about their relationship. She is saying that she has complete confidence in him; she trusts him.

Activity A

As a class, make a *belief* wall.

1. On pieces of card that are cut and coloured to look like bricks, write down some of your beliefs – things that you think are true, but cannot prove.
2. Include 'bricks' with religious beliefs on them.
3. Put the 'bricks' together to make a display.

Activity B

Think of someone you trust absolutely.

1. Make a list of the qualities and characteristics of that person.
2. Make another list of the feelings you have towards that person.

This person on the right means two things when she says 'I believe …':

1. I believe that God exists, and
2. I have complete trust and confidence in God.

I believe in God.

Belief and action

When people believe something strongly, they put their beliefs into action. Children who believe in fairies might put a fallen tooth under their pillow hoping it will be exchanged for money.

Religious people put their faith into action in a whole variety of ways. Worship is one way of doing it. A person's faith may influence them to spend their free time helping other people. The job they choose to do could be decided by faith. Some religious people will take leadership roles in their community. Others may become nurses, or teachers, or social workers so they can put their beliefs into practice. Others may focus on particular things they feel strongly about, and work to make others aware of them.

Activity C

1. In small groups, discuss why many people have a religious faith.
2. Then think of as many ways as you can how someone who believes in God might put their faith into action.
3. Draw a diagram like the one below, and insert your thoughts in the boxes.

Reason — **Faith** — **Actions**

Activity D

1. *'Faith is being sure of what we hope for and certain of what we do not see.'*
   This is a quotation from the Christian Bible. What do you think this means?
2. *'You can't base your life on uncertainty.'*
   Do you agree with this statement? You should refer to religious faith in your answer, and give reasons for your opinion.
3. Why might someone disagree with your answer to question 2 above?

2.4 What is religion?

Learning objectives

You will ...
- learn about the seven dimensions of religion
- apply the seven dimensions to your own social identity
- attempt to define religion.

We have seen that it is difficult to answer the question: Who am I? It is much easier to describe what you look like than to say who you are.

Professor Ninian Smart spent many years thinking about what religions look like. He decided that they have seven common features. He called them the **seven dimensions**.

Feelings Religions can bring about powerful feelings in people. They can make people feel happy and free, caring of others; they can inspire feelings of wonder and mystery.

Beliefs and teachings People who belong to a religion share the same beliefs about things like God, the meaning of life, how the universe came into being, and life after death.

Social Religious people tend to form groups with people with the same religious views. They may meet to study, worship or discuss their faith.

Rules All religions are clear about what is right and wrong, and how human beings should behave.

Material These are objects that are associated with the religion. They include special clothes, food, books and buildings.

Rituals Religions have special times, like festivals, and special services and ceremonies. Religious people may pray or meditate.

Stories Stories are used in religions to inspire people, to warn them against certain behaviours, or to explain difficult ideas.

Knowledge check

1. Copy the table below into your workbooks.
2. Match each of the following with the seven dimensions.

Adam and Eve   *Mosque*   *Passover*
Human beings are reborn after death
The Ten Commandments   *Joy*   *Roman Catholics*

Seven dimensions	Examples
Beliefs	
Stories	
Rules	
Rituals	
Feelings	
Social	
Material	

Most people who believe in God believe that God is:

omniscient – all knowing

omnipotent – all powerful

omnipresent – always present

omnibenevolent – perfectly good

immaterial – not physical

infinite – always existing from the past into the future.

Activity A

1. Think about the characteristics and qualities that believers say God has. If you could ask God five questions, what would they be?
2. Choose three of your questions. How would you answer them?

Activity B

1. What does the chart below show?
2. Look at the bars for the United Kingdom and those for the European Union as a whole.
   a. What are the main differences?
   b. What is similar?
   c. Is there anything that surprises you about this data?

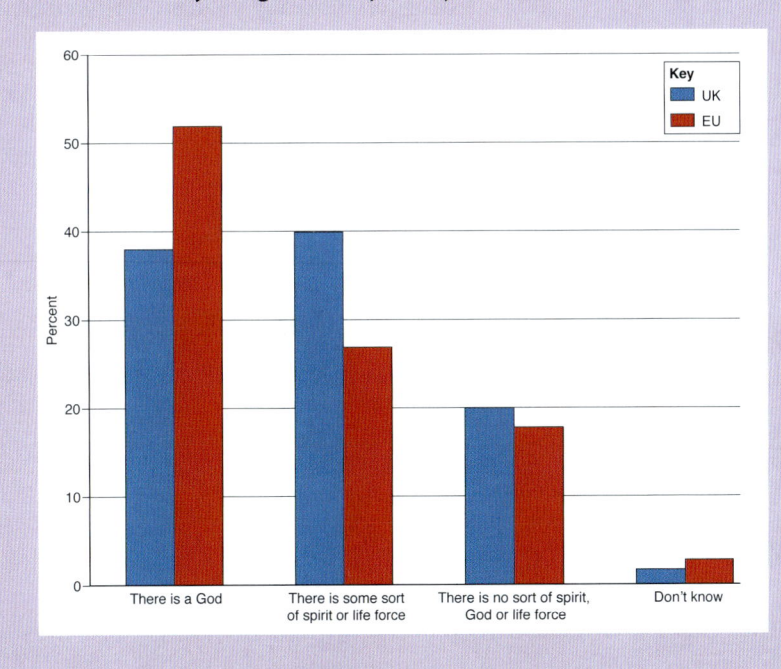

Knowledge check

1. What do the following words mean?
   a. omniscient
   b. omnipotent

2. Which one word can be used to mean:
   a. perfectly good
   b. always present?

What do religions believe about God?

Christianity, Islam and Judaism are called Abrahamic faiths, because their histories can all be traced back to one man, Abraham. Although they share a common root, there are many differences between them today.

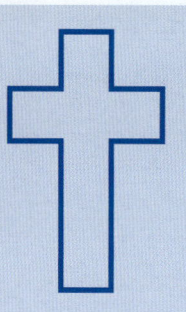

Christianity

Christians believe that there is one God who created the universe. They believe that God took the form of a human being, Jesus, about two thousand years ago, so ordinary humans can have a special relationship with him and be guided on how God wants them to live. Jesus is usually known as the Son of God. Christians believe that God lives in a spiritual way through human beings, so they can express their love for other beings. This idea of one God existing in three different ways – creator, human and spirit – is called the **Trinity**.

Judaism

Jews believe that there is one God who created the universe. They believe that they have a special, close relationship with God that has lasted through history. They believe that God guides them, like a father guides his children, and has done this through messengers or **prophets**. But the relationship carries with it heavy responsibilities to obey God's commands.

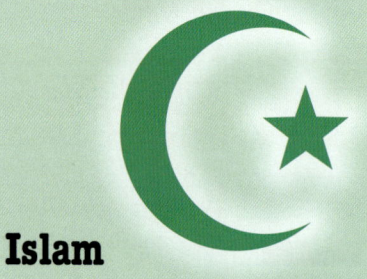

Islam

Muslims believe that there is one God who created the universe. God cannot be divided up and has no need to reproduce. They believe that nothing in the universe happens without God allowing it to happen. All beings depend on God for their existence, and learn about God from prophets – people who pass on guidance from God. Muhammad was the last and greatest of the prophets. Muslims often use the Arabic word **Allah**, which means The God, instead of just God.

Buddhism

Buddhists do not believe in a God who created the universe. Some Buddhists talk about **devas**, or heavenly beings, but they are not omniscient, omnipotent or omnipresent, so are not like other religions' ideas of God. In any case, most Buddhists see them as belonging to stories.

Sikhism

Sikhs believe in a single, personal God who creates everything. In a sense, God is everything. Sikhs try to develop a close relationship with God so that they can merge into God after death. They often refer to God as Waheguru, which means Wonderful Teacher.

Hinduism

Hinduism consists of a large number of different traditions. Each has a different idea of what God is like, so people often refer to a large number of gods in Hinduism. It might be more accurate to say that, for Hindus, there is one God that can be experienced in many different forms. Hindus tend to be attached to one particular form. Hindus believe that God creates the universe, sustains it, and destroys it in an infinite cycle.

Activity C

Using the information from this chapter, and your own research, compare Jewish, Christian and Islamic ideas about God.

1. Note down the ideas that are common to the three religions.
2. Then outline what is unique to each of them.

Activity D

The names that different religions use for God tell you a lot about their beliefs. For example, Jews and Christians refer to God as *Father*; Muslims never do. Yet Muslims have 99 other names for God.

1. Conduct some research into the names for God in different religions.
2. Present your findings to the rest of your class either as a display or as a presentation.

2.6 What is life?

Learning objectives

You will …
- learn about the major religions' teachings about human life
- compare the teachings of different religions
- reflect on how you can influence your future.

All of the world's major religions, except Buddhism, teach that God created the universe and life, including human life.

Judaism, Christianity and Islam

Judaism and Christianity teach that God created human beings 'in his own image'.

Creating human beings 'in his own image' does not mean that people look like God. For Jews, it means that human beings are able to think for themselves and make choices.

Christians understand this to mean that all human beings have God's goodness in them.

The holy books of Judaism, Christianity and Islam all tell a separate story of God creating the first human beings, Adam and Eve. The story describes not only how God made the first human being, but also how God gave him life: he breathed life into him. The story goes on to describe how the couple disobeyed God.

Jews take this to mean that God created human beings to think for themselves and make choices. They believe that God made them to have a conscience, so they know right from wrong. They believe that God also gave them instincts, like the desires to eat, drink and have families. Sometimes, humans make wise choices; sometimes, they don't.

Christians believe that the story of Adam and Eve disobeying God explains that all human beings fall short of the high standards God has for them. Some say that this is how death became a feature of human life.

Islam teaches that, after disobeying God, Adam and Eve begged for God's forgiveness. God forgave them, and this explains that all human beings are in a state of **submission** to God, which means they have a duty to obey him.

The holy books of Judaism, Christianity and Islam teach that God created human beings with the freedom to choose how to act.

Hinduism, Sikhism and Buddhism

Hindus, Buddhists and Sikhs all believe that the good and bad things people do will be repaid to them. They call this karma. After death, people are reborn in the world to continue to live through the results of their actions.

Sikhism teaches that living a good life will lead to a happy rebirth. The only way out of the cycle is to become one with God.

For Hindus, Brahman (God) is behind all things. Brahman is in all things, and all things are Brahman. They believe that Brahman is deep within all beings. They believe that people can escape from living in the world to become one with Brahman.

Buddhists do not believe in a God that created life. Living in the world cannot bring true happiness, because the things that bring us happiness can change or disappear: in the end, they make us unhappy and we suffer. Buddhism teaches that if people do not rely on things to make them happy, then they cannot be disappointed.

This symbol is pronounced Om. It is special to Hindus for whom it means God and Everything that is.

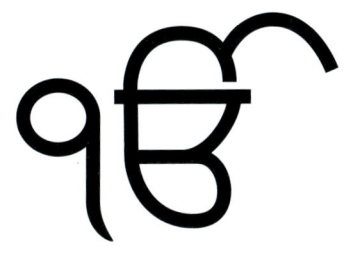

This symbol is pronounced Ik Onkar. It is based on the Om of Hinduism, and means One God. It is used by Sikhs.

Knowledge check

Read pages 44–45.

1. Which religions teach that human beings were made in the image of God?
2. Which religions teach that human beings disobeyed God?
3. Which religion teaches that human beings are in a state of submission to God?
4. Which religion teaches that everything is God?
5. What is karma?
6. Which religions believe in karma?
7. Which religion does not teach that God created human beings?

45

Activity A

Hinduism, Buddhism and Sikhism all teach that whatever happens to you in your life is caused by things you have done in the past. This means that if you are careful about what you do now, you can make the future whatever you want it to be.

1. What would you want your life to be like in the future, and why?
2. What can you do now to make it happen?

Some Buddhists show their beliefs about life in pictures called *The Wheel of Life*.

46

Activity B

1. Look carefully at the picture of *The Wheel of Life* opposite. For Buddhists it shows what life is like.

2. With a partner, see if you can find the following things:
   - people showing anger
   - people being greedy
   - people being happy
   - people suffering
   - birth
   - death.

3. Now collect pictures from newspapers and magazines to make a collage of your own wheel of life.

Activity C

1. Draw a beliefs web. You can use the one below as a starting point. Copy it out into your workbooks.

2. Start by putting the names of the major religions in circles.

3. Use the information on these pages to select religious beliefs about human nature, and put them into rectangles. Draw lines to connect them up.

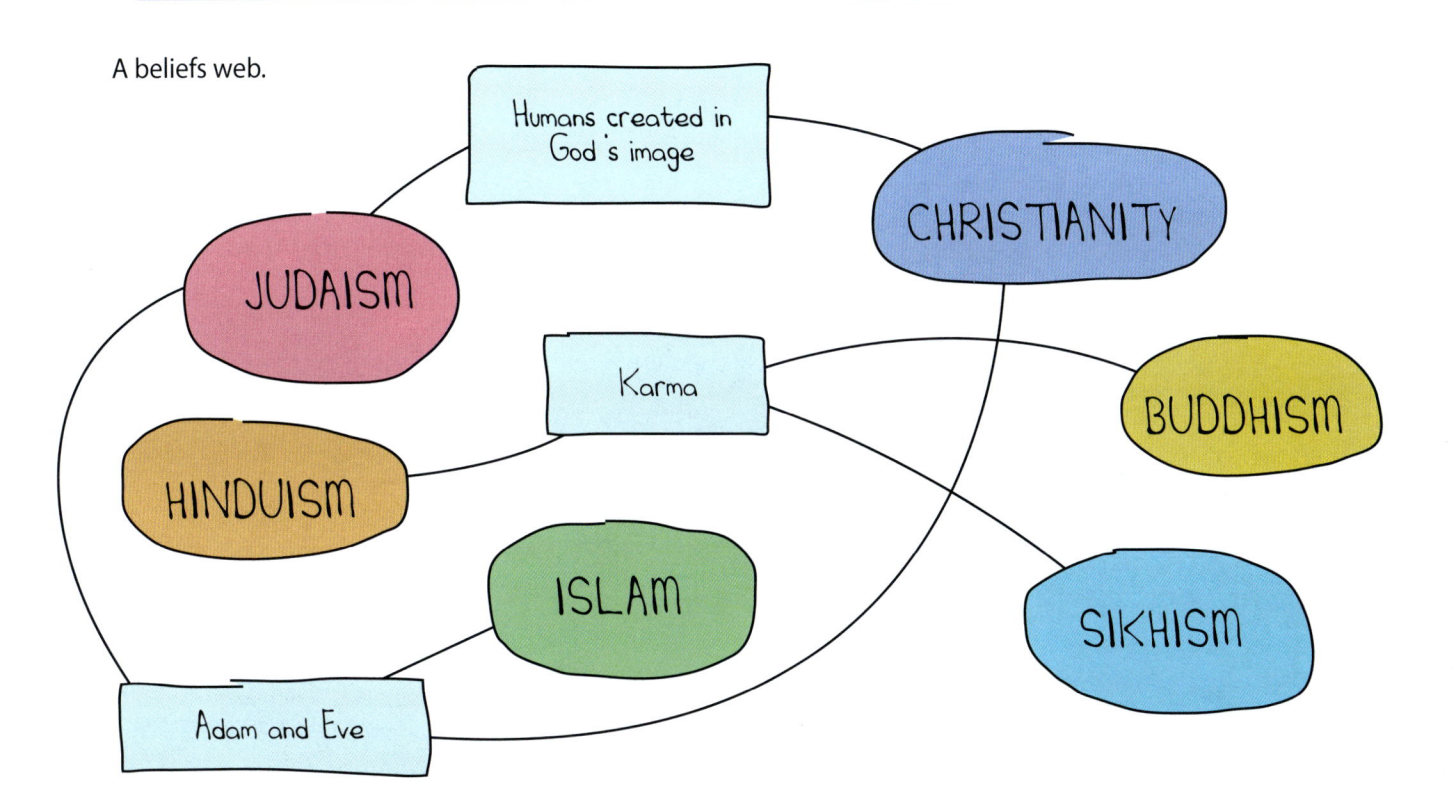

A beliefs web.

[Diagram showing a beliefs web with circles labelled JUDAISM, CHRISTIANITY, HINDUISM, BUDDHISM, ISLAM, SIKHISM connected by lines to rectangles labelled "Humans created in God's image", "Karma", and "Adam and Eve".]

Activity D

1. Choose one of the six major religions. Use a variety of resources to create a presentation about that religion's teachings about human nature.

2. How do those teachings affect the life of a believer in the twenty-first century?

2.7 Did the universe have a beginning?

Learning objectives

You will …
- learn about scientific views about the origin of the universe
- understand different religious accounts about the origin of the universe
- compare views about the origins of the universe
- consider the importance of learning about different views.

The earliest religions attempted to explain how and why the universe came about. As people became more and more certain about how the universe began, they called the new knowledge **science**.

According to science, the Big Bang expanded to create the universe.

What science says

1 Time and space started with a small ball of infinite density – a singularity.

2 The singularity exploded – the **Big Bang**. It let loose a huge amount of energy, which travelled away from it.

3 As the energy expanded, the amount of space got bigger and bigger. Particles of energy came together to form matter – the gases, liquids and solids that make up the universe.

4 The universe is still expanding today.

What Judaism and Christianity say

Judaism and Christianity teach that the universe was created by God. According to the Bible story, God made it in six days from nothing.

Some Jews and Christians believe that God made the universe in six days – exactly as the Bible says.

Most Jews and Christians believe that God made the Big Bang happen.

This painting is called *The Ancient of Days*, and was painted by William Blake. It is sometimes called *God as Architect*. It shows God using mathematical instruments to design the universe. Blake is trying to show that there is order in the chaos of the universe.

Activity A

1 Find out more details about what the Bible and Hindu teachings say about the origins of the universe. What do they agree about?

2 What differences are there?

49

What Hinduism says

Hinduism teaches that the universe is not created once, but repeatedly, so that universes existed before this one. It also teaches that other universes exist at the same time as this one.

The universe was created from nothing.

Energy in the form of sound caused the universe to expand. The sound can be pronounced 'Om' or 'Aum'.

Activity B

1. Find out more details about what the Bible and Hindu teachings say about the origins of the universe. Find out also about the Big Bang theory.
2. Compare religious views about the creation of the universe with scientific ones.

The beginning of the universe is sometimes represented by an egg in Hindu art. The egg is a singularity from which the universe grows.

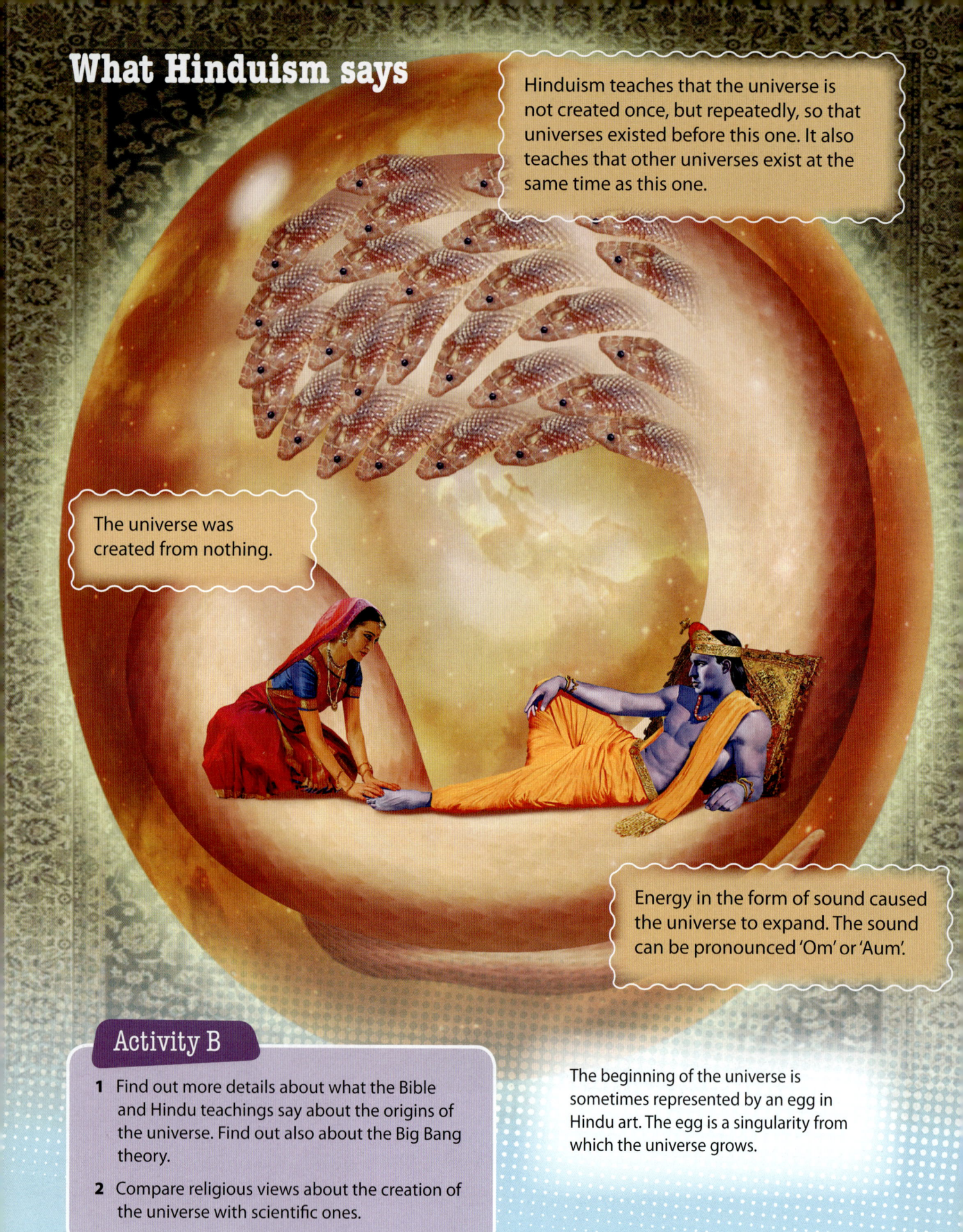

Creationism

Experts Call for Creationism in the Classroom

Creationism – the belief that life came into existence thousands of years ago as described in the Bible or the Qur'an, rather than millions of years ago, which scientists believe – is on the rise in the UK.

This makes the teaching of the scientific theories a problem in some schools.

But academics from the Institute of Education in London and Valdosta State University in the US say the theory of evolution should be taught as a significant part of science lessons, with room to discuss creationism.

And yesterday, the Council of Europe (CoE) urged governments to 'firmly oppose' the teaching of creationism as a scientific discipline.

A spokesman for the Department for Children, Schools and Families (DCSF) [in England] said creationism should not be taught in science lessons.

'Guidance for schools and teachers, published today, makes it clear that creationism is not a recognised scientific theory, and therefore must not be taught as fact in science classes,' he said.

Adapted from an article in the *Education Guardian*, 5 October 2007

Activity C

Read the newspaper article on the rise of creationism.

1 What reasons do the academics from London and Valdosta State University have for saying that creationism should be taught in science lessons in schools?
2 Why are the Council of Europe and the DCSF against it?
3 What is your view, and why?

> Looking in the Bible for a scientific account of origins is like looking in the phone directory for a recipe for angel cake.

Tom Harpur (Canadian writer on religion and spirituality).

Activity D

Read the opinion on creationism in the speech bubble.

1 Explain in your own words what Tom Harpur is saying.
2 What reasons might he have for putting forward this point of view?
3 Read the biblical story of the creation (Genesis 1). If it is not supposed to be a theory about how the universe was created, what is it about?

2.8 Will the universe have an end?

> **Learning objectives**
> You will...
> - learn about some scientific theories about the possible end of the universe
> - compare scientific theories with Hindu teachings
> - compare teachings of the Abrahamic faiths about the end of time
> - think about how good can come out of evil.

What science says

Here are three scientific theories about what may happen to the universe in the future.

The Big Freeze
As the universe expands, it gets colder and colder – too cold for any life form to exist.

The Big Rip
The expansion of the universe gets faster and faster until everything in it rips apart.

The Big Crunch
The expansion of the universe slows to a stop. Then it contracts back into a singularity ready for another Big Bang.

Religions use the word **eschatology** (meaning *study of the last things*) to describe beliefs about the end of time.

Hinduism

Hinduism teaches that the universe is created, expands and dies. These three phases are represented by aspects of God, known as the **Trimurti**.

Brahma creates the universe from a golden egg. Energy from the sound of Om expands into empty darkness.

Vishnu is the preserver and protector of the universe. He appears on Earth in troubled times to restore the balance between good and evil.

At the end of Brahma's lifetime, **Shiva** comes to destroy the universe so that it can be recreated by a new Brahma after a period of rest.

Activity A

1. Which scientific theory about the end of the universe most closely matches Hindu teachings?
2. Explain your answer.

Judaism, Christianity, Islam

The Abrahamic faiths associate the end of time with the creation of a new age in which people will live under God's authority.

For Jews, at the end of this age, God will appoint a king who will lead the Jewish people in an age of peace. This religious king is known as the **Messiah**.

Christians believe the Messiah has already appeared, in the form of Jesus Christ (Christ means Messiah).

In Islam, on the Day of Judgement, the dead will rise, and Allah will judge each person according to their actions in life.

The Christian Bible teaches that Jesus will come again at the end of time. The dead will return to life, and all people will be judged according to how well they have led their lives.

Some Jews believe that the dead will be reawakened when the Messiah comes.

Activity B

Look carefully at the picture of the Trimurti on page 53.

1. Which representation of God is Brahma, which is Vishnu, and which is Shiva?
2. What symbols are there that show Brahma's creative powers?
3. How does the artist show that Vishnu keeps the universe going?
4. How is Shiva shown to be the destroyer?

Look at the painting *Der Weg Zum Paradies* on page 55.

5. Look carefully at the people in the picture. What sort of people are travelling to Christ's kingdom?
6. What sort of people are moving to eternal torture?

Si tu hais le péché, de la croix charge toi,
Marche avec courage, soutenu par ta foi,
Suis moi sur le chemin pierreux, plein d'épines,
Qui te conduit au Ciel aux délices divines.

Si tu crains ici-bas, les soucis, la fatigue,
Et te ris des conseils, que ton Dieu te prodigue,
Prends le chemin facile des plaisirs matériels,

Der Weg Zum Paradies – an unknown artist's vision of what the Christian Day of Judgement may look like.

Activity C

Shiva represents a god of violence and destruction; yet it is through his actions that a new universe can be created.

1. Think of a situation when an event that appeared to be negative or destructive paved the way for something good to happen.
2. Can you think how Shiva reflects the natural world?

Read Matthew 25:31–46 from the Bible.

3. How is the painting above different from the description of judgement in the Bible?
4. Why do you think the artist has portrayed it differently?

Activity D

Conduct some research into scientific theories about the end of the universe and other religious teachings about it. Write an article entitled *How can religious people believe science?*

1. You will need to find out about scientific theories about the origins and future of the universe, and also what the religions teach.
2. You will need to take into account the fact that not all people of the same faith agree about its teachings.

The big assignment

Task
To present the views of members of your community on religion and personal values.

Outcome
Either produce a PowerPoint® presentation or make a class display of your findings.

Objectives
- To find out whether your friends and family are religious.
- To find out about the beliefs, values and objects that are precious to them.
- To discover if there is a worldview that your community shares.

An example of a typical community.

Guidance

Work in groups of four or five; then put together the results of your survey so you have more information to work with.

Your first job is to write the questions you are going to include in your survey. You want to find out from the people you ask:

- **a** what they mean by 'religion'
- **b** whether they think they are religious
- **c** whether they believe in God
- **d** whether they believe there is life after death
- **e** whether they believe life has a purpose
- **f** what rules are most important to them
- **g** what values are important to them
- **h** whether they have special places they like to go, and where they are
- **i** who they most admire
- **j** which groups they belong to.

Add some more ideas of your own.

Before you write your questions, make sure you revise the seven dimensions of religion in Chapter 2.4, pages 38–39.

1. Each person in the group should survey five people – friends and family. Decide in advance who is going to ask whom, so that you don't all target the same people. You should also include your own views.

2. When you have completed the survey, get together again to compare your results. Analyse the answers to each question, noting which answers occur more than once. Try to write an answer table, with the most popular answers at the top.

3. Think about how you will present your data. Will it be in bar charts, or tables, or pie charts? Will you make a display, or an electronic presentation?

4. Discuss what the data mean. Do they give you an idea of the kinds of beliefs and values that are shared in your community?

5. Try to organise your data under the headings of the seven dimensions.

6. Compare your results with other groups.

Assessment

You will be assessed on:

- ✓ how well you use specialist vocabulary
- ✓ how you compare different people's responses
- ✓ how you relate people's responses to the seven dimensions.

3.1 How do we know right from wrong?

Learning objectives

You will …
- learn about what a conscience is
- understand some religious views about conscience
- express personal viewpoints on issues of right and wrong
- analyse and evaluate a range of views about what is right and wrong.

A **conscience** is a sense of what is right and wrong.

- Some **psychologists** think that human beings are born knowing the difference between right and wrong. They call this a conscience.
- Some people think a conscience develops as we get older.
- Some people think the conscience tells us after we have done something whether it is right or wrong. If it is wrong, we feel guilty; if it is right, we feel good.
- Some people think the conscience tells us in advance whether what we are about to do is right or wrong. Then we choose.

Some thoughts on conscience:

> Conscience is a man's compass.

Vincent van Gogh, painter.

> A good conscience is a continual Christmas.

Benjamin Franklin, one of the Founding Fathers of the United States of America.

> A clear and innocent conscience fears nothing.

Elizabeth I, Queen of England.

> There is no witness so terrible, no accuser so powerful as conscience which lives inside us.

Sophocles, ancient Greek playwright.

> Conscience is God present in man.

Victor Hugo, French writer.

> There is a higher court than courts of justice and that is the court of conscience.

Mahatma Gandhi, leader of the Indian movement for independence.

Knowledge check

1. Choose three of the quotations about conscience.
2. Try to put them into your own words.

What do the religions say?

Hindus believe that we have many lives, during which we get to know the difference between right and wrong. This knowledge is our conscience.

Buddhism says that conscience is loving kindness for all living beings which can grow stronger through determined effort.

Islam teaches that God plants the knowledge of right and wrong in each person, but people have free choice to do what they want. This means that people will have to answer to God for what they have done wrong.

Christians believe that the knowledge of good and bad is part of human nature, created by God; but, to help them make the right choices, people need rules as well.

In a nutshell …
- Some people believe the conscience is a function of the mind that people are born with.
- Some people believe that the conscience is just a developing knowledge of what is right and wrong.
- Some people believe that conscience makes you feel guilty after you have done something wrong.
- Some people believe the conscience is a warning that happens before you do something wrong.

Right or wrong?

1. A friend copies music/a game/some software from another friend.

2. A man promises his dying mother he will visit her grave every day when she dies. After her death, he never visits her grave.

3. A friend smokes cigarettes. You promise not to tell her parents. Yet, when her mother asks you outright, you tell her.

4. You promise your pet dog that, if he dies, you will never replace him, because you could never love a pet as much as you love him. Your dog is run over and killed. After two months, you get a puppy and find you love it as much as you loved your previous dog.

5. A person in your school steals a CD from a shop.

6. You have not done your science homework. Your friend, who is in a different group from you, has been set the same homework and has done it. He says you can copy it, and you do.

7. You have a really important maths exam tomorrow. You find a copy of the question paper in the corridor: your maths teacher has evidently dropped it. You take it and put it in your bag.

8 Your maths teacher is late to your lesson, and you discover that she has left tomorrow's question papers on her desk. You take one and put it in your bag.

9 A friend steals a CD from the bag of a boy in your class who neither of you like. He burns a copy and offers it to you.

Activity A

1 Read through the nine scenarios. Decide whether the action taken in each case is right or wrong.

2 Compare your answers with a friend's.

Activity B

1 Read through the nine scenarios on pages 60–61. For each one, say whether you think the action taken is right, wrong or in between. Try to give a reason for each of your decisions.

2 Now discuss your answers with a partner. Which decisions and reasons do you agree about? Which do you disagree about? Try to persuade your partner to accept your point of view.

Activity C

Use the nine scenarios to conduct a survey of whether people in your school think the action taken is right, wrong or in between.

1 For each scenario, ask your interviewee to give a brief reason for their answer.

2 Try to survey a range of people – pupils, teaching assistants, other support staff and teachers.

3 At the end of each interview, ask the following questions:

How old are you? 11–14 15–16 17–19 20–30 over 30
Are you religious? Yes No

4 Use the responses to answer the following questions:

 a Do people's views about what is right and what is wrong depend on their age?
 b Do people's views about what is right and what is wrong differ according to their religious beliefs?

Activity D

1 Conduct a survey as described in Activity C.

2 Use the results to write a report on how people decide what is right and wrong. You should also give your own opinions on how far you agree with other people's views.

61

3.2 What makes something good?

Learning objectives

You will …
- learn how some religions define what is good
- understand what religions teach about how to act righteously
- interpret some religious statements
- present your own point of view about what is good.

Guiding principles

Religions have general principles to help human beings know what is right and good or wrong and bad.

Buddhism

Whatever is motivated by greed, anger or stupidity is wrong.

Whatever is motivated by wisdom, compassion or generosity is right.

Hinduism

Whatever is rooted in **ahimsa** is good. Ahimsa means *the avoidance of violence towards any living being*. It also means having respect for every living being.

Some religions have lists of rules or commandments for proper behaviour, for example:

Judaism

Respect your father and mother.
Do not commit murder.
Do not commit adultery.
Do not steal.
Do not tell lies about other people.
Do not be jealous of what other people have.

Religions also have guidelines for living throughout their holy literature, for example:

Sikhism

Work hard and work with honesty.
Lead a truthful life.
Help the needy and the poor.
Love your children.
Respect your parents.
Do not harm others.
Do not discriminate on the basis of colour, religion, class and creed.
Do not take alcohol, tobacco or drugs.
Do not steal.
Do not gamble.

Activity A

1 Look again at what ahimsa means in Hinduism. How would basing your life on ahimsa affect the way you live?
2 Think about what your attitudes to the following would be:

   war   the environment   what you eat   what you wear

3 Compare your ideas with someone else's, and together make a poster to show how ahimsa could be put into practice in daily life.

Religious views on issues

1 Sikhism

He who restores a thing to its rightful owner ... shall be blessed with four times the reward.

2 Sikhism

In the company of bad people, one faces great sorrows.

3 Islam

Fight in the cause of Allah those who fight you, but do not go beyond this limit.

4 Buddhism

Avoid taking alcohol and drugs because they cloud the mind.

5
Christianity

You have heard that it was said to the people long ago, 'Do not murder, and anyone who murders will be subject to judgement.' But I tell you that anyone who is angry with his brother will be subject to judgement.

6
Christianity

You have heard that it was said, 'Do not commit adultery.' But I tell you that anyone who looks at a woman lustfully has already committed adultery with her in his heart.

Activity B

1. Look at the statements on pages 64–65. Each comes from a holy book and presents a religious view on an issue.
2. Discuss the statements with a partner. For each one, write down what it means.
3. Then say whether you agree with it or not, or agree to some extent. Give reasons for your answers.
4. Try to give reasons why some people may have a different point of view.

Activity C

All religions teach that violence towards other human beings is wrong; yet some of their followers have used violence, and some still do.

1. Find out why some religious people sometimes accept violence, and in which circumstances. What is your view?
2. You could present your work as an e-presentation.

Activity D

What do you think makes something good, or the right thing to do?

1. Write a report that outlines religious points of view.
2. Then compare these views with your own.

3.3 What is the Golden Rule?

Learning objectives

You will …
- learn what the Golden Rule is
- understand different versions of the Golden Rule in different religions
- apply the Golden Rule to a range of situations

The religions of the world have tried to summarise their teachings on what is good and right. The words they use are different, but the meaning is the same. It is called the **Golden Rule**. It helps people decide what is right in many situations.

Bahá'í

Lay not on any soul a load that you would not wish to be laid upon you, and desire not for anyone the things you would not desire for yourself.
(Bahá'u'lláh, *Gleanings*)

Buddhism

Treat not others in ways that you yourself would find hurtful.
(The Buddha, *Udana-Varga* 5.18)

Christianity

In everything, do to others as you would have them do to you; for this is the law and the **prophets**.
(Jesus, *Matthew* 7:12)

Hinduism

This is the sum of duty: do not do to others what would cause pain if done to you.
(*Mahabharata* 5:1517)

Islam

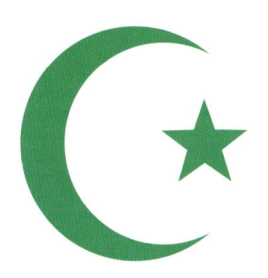

Not one of you truly believes until you wish for others what you wish for yourself.
(The Prophet Muhammad, Hadith)

Judaism

What is hateful to you, do not do to your neighbour. This is the whole Torah; all the rest is commentary. Go and learn it.
(Hillel, Talmud, Shabbath 31a)

Sikhism

I am a stranger to no one; and no one is a stranger to me. Indeed, I am a friend to all.
(Guru Granth Sahib, p.1299)

Taoism

Regard your neighbour's gain as your own gain and your neighbour's loss as your own loss.
(Lao Tzu, T'ai Shang Kan Ying P'ien, 213–218)

Zoroastrianism

Do not do unto others whatever is injurious to yourself.
(Shayast-na-Shayast 13.29)

Activity A

1. Read through the different versions of the Golden Rule on pages 66–67. Choose three that you would like to display on a poster.
2. Find some pictures of people putting the Golden Rule into practice to add to your poster.

The following statements look like they may be examples of the Golden Rule, but they are not.

1 A mentally ill person who hurts others so others will hurt them.

2 Doing to others the bad things that they did to you first.

3 Doing to others what you think they would do to you if they had the chance.

4 Using 'an eye for an eye, a tooth for a tooth' as a guide when mistreated.

5 Giving someone a present in the hope that they will give you a more expensive one.

What is golden about the Golden Rule?

Gold is a powerful symbol in all cultures and throughout history. It represents what is great in human activity; it points to the most pure, most noble and most precious parts of human experience.

Until fairly recently, gold was the most valuable of all metals. Although today there are other metals that fetch higher prices, gold still keeps its power as a metaphor.

Gold is used as a symbol in a number of religious traditions.
- Some statues of the **Buddha** and the roofs of some Buddhist temples are made of gold or covered in gold leaf.
- The Harmandir Sahib, pictured opposite, is the most important of all Sikh temples. It is known as the Golden Temple.

Activity B

1. Read through the statements above.
2. For each one, say why they are not examples of the Golden Rule.

'To become gold is to become light, and the light in this precise sense is Truth itself.'
(Hazrat Inayat Khan, nineteenth-century Muslim teacher.)

Activity C

1. Write a list of ten guidelines for behaviour in your school based on the Golden Rule.
2. Compare your list with some of your classmates. Between you, can you come up with a list that your teacher would agree with?

The proper name of the Golden Temple is the Harmandir Sahib, which means the Holy Temple of God. It is situated in the city of Amritsar in the Punjab.

Activity D

1. Can you think of situations when following the Golden Rule may not be the best course of action?
2. For each situation you can think of, explain why not, and suggest better ways of handling it.

3.4 What is a moral dilemma?

Learning objectives

You will …
- learn about what a moral dilemma is
- understand why moral dilemmas can be hard to solve
- analyse the kinds of factors that have to be taken into account when trying to solve a moral dilemma.

If you have to make a choice between stealing something and not stealing it is, in most cases, easy to decide what is the right thing to do (even if you don't do it). But most decisions are harder to make. Consider the case of Mrs Franklin.

Mrs Franklin and her cats

You are in a supermarket on a busy Saturday afternoon. Among all the people there, you recognise one old lady, Mrs Franklin. She lives near you, and has a reputation for being rather strange. She lives on her own in a shabby house with a number of cats.

Her story is well known. Both her husband and their only son were killed in a car crash some 30 years before. She fell apart, and has never recovered. She cut herself off from the world, devoting all her love and attention to the family's pet cats. As the years passed, the cats grew in number, and the old lady became more and more eccentric. She has very little money and lives in squalor. What little she has, she prefers to spend on her beloved cats than herself.

As you watch old Mrs Franklin, you see her pick up a tin of cat food and put it in her pocket. She clearly intends to leave the store without paying for it.

What do you do?

It seems whatever you do, something good will happen and something bad will happen. This kind of situation is called a **moral dilemma**.

The problem with moral dilemmas is that doing what is right can result in something that is wrong. On the other hand, doing what is wrong can produce something good.

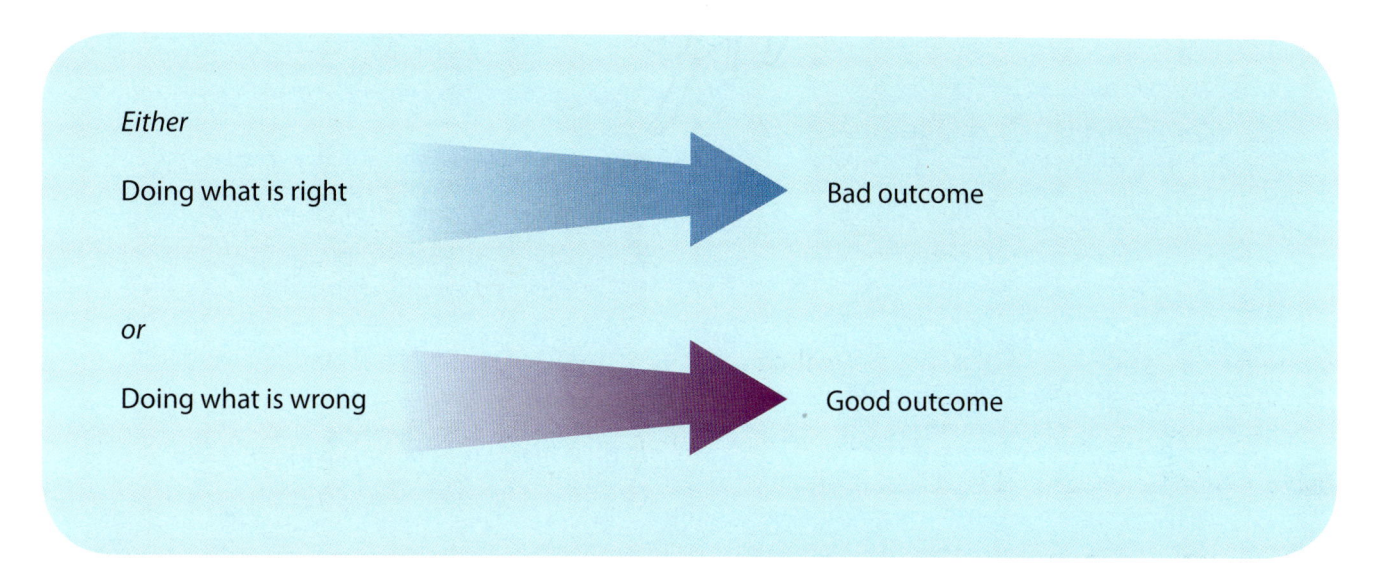

Either

Doing what is right → Bad outcome

or

Doing what is wrong → Good outcome

In a moral dilemma, it is not possible to do the right thing and guarantee a good outcome.

Activity A

Draw up the moral dilemma of Mrs Franklin on a storyboard.

1. Divide an A3 sheet into eight panels.
2. Draw a scene in each of the first six panels, with a caption to explain what is happening.
3. Use the last two panels to draw and caption how you think the story should end. What would you do, and what would the consequences be?

Activity B

1. Discuss the story of Mrs Franklin with a partner. List all the options that are open to you.
2. Then for each one, describe what the likely consequences would be – both good and bad.

Would it make any difference to Mrs Franklin's story if:

A ... Mrs Franklin was stealing from a small family-run grocer, not a big supermarket chain?

B ... Mrs Franklin could afford to buy the cat food?

C ... Mrs Franklin had not had a breakdown?

D ... Mrs Franklin was stealing food for herself?

E ... you could be punished if it is found that you knew about the theft but did not report it?

F ... Mrs Franklin was stealing an mp3 player?

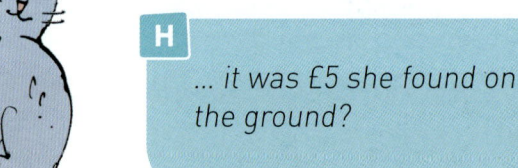

G ... Mrs Franklin could have her hand cut off if she was found guilty?

H ... it was £5 she found on the ground?

I ... you didn't like Mrs Franklin?

J ... Mrs Franklin had been prosecuted for shoplifting a year ago?

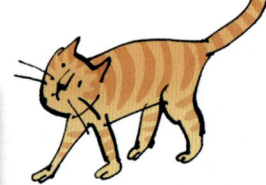

K ... Mrs Franklin had living relatives?

L ... you were religious?

M ... you were not religious?

N ... Mrs Franklin was religious?

Activity C

1. Complete Activity B. Now discuss the questions in Would it make a difference? and record your answers.

2. Then think about and answer the following questions.

   a In this situation, which of the possible courses of action would be:
   - best for Mrs Franklin?
   - best for you?
   - best for the supermarket?
   - best for society?

   b Which of these (the welfare of Mrs Franklin, your welfare, that of the supermarket and that of society) is most important? Why?

   c Is the welfare of the cats an important factor to consider?

3. How might a religious person answer all these questions?

This is part of the story of *Les Miserables*, a novel by Victor Hugo, which is also a musical.

Jean Valjean is a poor man living in hard times. His parents are dead, so he lives with his sister and her seven children. He is unable to support the family, so one day he steals some bread from a baker's shop. He is caught and sentenced to five years in prison.

While in prison, Valjean tries many times to escape, but is caught on each occasion. His sentence is increased to nineteen years.

When he is finally released, Valjean is on parole: if he commits another crime, he will face life in prison. He can get no work, and no one will give him accommodation. He breaks into the house of a bishop and steals some silver. He is caught and brought back to the bishop. The bishop saves him from arrest by claiming that the silver was a gift; he even gives Valjean some more silver.

In spite of possessing the silver, Valjean steals some money from a poor boy. Later, he feels guilty, and tries to find the child, but the theft has been reported. Valjean is now on the run for breaking his parole.

Valjean settles down and changes his name. He becomes a wealthy factory owner, the mayor of his town, and helps a lot of people through charitable works. He learns that a homeless man has been identified as Jean Valjean and arrested. The real Valjean does not know what to do. If he gives himself up, an innocent man will be freed. On the other hand, Valjean himself will be arrested. The people who rely on him will suffer. In any case, the tramp may have a better life in prison than on the streets …

Activity D

1. Go through the story of Jean Valjean. Highlight each of the moral dilemmas, and indicate the choices Valjean had.
2. Imagine that he had made different choices with different consequences. Rewrite the story to reflect these changes.

3.5 How can you solve a moral dilemma?

Learning objectives

You will...
- learn about the six steps of solving moral dilemmas
- understand how religious ideas can be applied to moral dilemmas
- give examples of religious moral decision making.

Moral dilemmas

1 You want to buy a designer T-shirt that costs £20. The sales assistant misreads the label and asks you for £10.

Do you tell the sales assistant that he has made a mistake?

2 Two of your friends come to your house to watch TV. When they leave, you find £5 on the sofa. It may be yours, but you're not sure.

Do you ask your friends if it belongs to one of them?

3 In your first week at secondary school you meet Alex and the two of you become friends. When you tell your parents about Alex, they are horrified. They know Alex's family and don't like them, but they won't tell you why. They forbid you from seeing Alex.

Do you obey your parents?

4 A friend of yours, Sam, is being bullied by some older pupils in the school, and is very frightened because the bullies are very intimidating. The ringleader knows you are a friend of Sam's and wants to have a fight with you. The ringleader doesn't know you are a martial arts expert.

Do you protect Sam by fighting the ringleader?

Activity A

1. Choose one or two of the moral dilemmas on pages 74–75.
2. With a partner, work through the six steps of solving a moral dilemma on page 76.
3. Make notes on your discussion at each step. What is your final decision?
4. Which of the dilemmas was the most difficult to solve? Why?

Solving moral dilemmas

It is not easy to solve moral dilemmas. But if you use some of the knowledge and skills you have learnt over the last few lessons, it may become easier. Here are some steps you could take.

1. What are the options? Do you or don't you? Are there any other possibilities?

2. Remember the Golden Rule. Try not to think about what is best for you. Think about what is better in the long term for the other people involved.

3. Think about rules and guidelines about right and wrong. Jews and some Christians try to follow the Ten Commandments. Buddhists have the Five Precepts. What rules do you have? If you are a religious person, what does your religion teach? If you are not religious, what rules or guidelines have you been taught?

4. Think about the consequences. For each possibility you can think of, consider what may happen to each of the people involved.

5. What does your conscience tell you? If you have made a decision about what to do, do you have a feeling that it is right?

6. Check with someone else. Ask someone whose opinion you trust whether they agree with your decision. A religious person might ask a fellow-believer or a religious leader.

Stages for solving moral dilemmas.

Activity B

Complete Activity A on page 75. Then write your own moral dilemma. It could be something that really happened to you or someone you know, or it could be made up. Give it to your partner to solve using the six steps.

Activity C

Complete Activity A on page 75. Then for your chosen moral dilemma, look at step 3 of the stages for solving a moral dilemma for different religions. What solutions do the different religions come up with? Use examples to explain your answer.

A painful problem

You may have heard people say things like, 'I don't know what to buy Laura for her birthday. It's a real dilemma.' The word dilemma is often used to mean any problem, but its meaning is really much more precise than that.

The 'di' bit of the word means two, and a 'lemma' is a statement that is assumed to be true. So a dilemma is a problem that has two possible solutions. In a real dilemma, both options involve something bad. This is why they are sometimes called the horns of the dilemma. Like the horns of a bull, you don't want to get caught on either of them.

So, what if you have a problem with more than two possible, but undesirable, solutions? There are words for them, but they are hardly ever used.

Trilemma – three bad options

Tetralemma – four bad options

Pentalemma – five bad options

Polylemma – lots of bad options

Activity D

Complete Activity C. Is it easier for religious people to solve moral dilemmas? Explain your answer by giving examples.

3.6 What is love?

Learning objectives

You will ...
- learn what religions teach about love
- compare religious definitions of love
- analyse what love means to religious people.

Religions teach that people have a duty to do right and live good lives. This is because they believe that love is what should motivate them in whatever they do.

Buddhism

In Buddhism the word **metta** means loving-kindness. Buddhists practise metta by:
- not hating any other being
- not offending any other being
- not harming any other being
- not killing any other being
- not annoying any other being
- wishing metta to all other beings.

Not only does metta bring happiness to others, it comes back to you:

You sleep easily, wake easily, dream no evil dreams. You are valued by human beings, valued by non-human beings. You are protected from harm. Fire, poison, or weapons cannot touch you. Your mind gains concentration quickly. Your face is bright. You will die unconfused.

(Anguttara Nikaya 11.16)

Some Buddhists hang up prayer flags so that happiness can spread with the wind to all beings.

Knowledge check

1. What does metta mean?
2. Give two ways that Buddhists can put metta into practice.

Christianity

For Christians, love is given to human beings by God. Human beings should love each other in the same way that God loves them. This kind of love is called **agape**.

Let us love one another, for love comes from God. Everyone who loves has been born of God and knows God. Whoever does not love does not know God, because God is love.
(1 John 4:7–8)

Here is a definition of agape from the Bible:

Love is patient; love is kind. It does not envy, it does not boast, it is not proud. It is not rude, it is not self-seeking, it is not easily angered, it keeps no record of wrongs. Love does not delight in evil but rejoices with the truth. It always protects, always trusts, always hopes, always perseveres.
(1 Corinthians 13.4–7)

The logo of Agape Unlimited, an American Christian charity that provides medical care for isolated communities in the Arctic and Siberia.

Hinduism

Hindus use the word ahimsa to describe the way they should treat other beings. Ahimsa means 'doing no harm'. Hindus believe that all beings are part of God, so harming another being, including animals, means harming yourself. This is how karma works.

Do not kill those who are capable of being fathers and mothers.
(from the Rig Veda)

Knowledge check

1. For which religion is agape important?
2. Where do human beings receive agape from?

Islam

In Islam, love is a word that particularly describes the relationship between human beings and Allah. Human beings should love Allah more than any human being.

Among people there are those who take others to be equal to Allah. They love them as they would love Allah. But those who have faith love Allah more than anything else.

(Qur'an 2:165)

Judaism

Ahava in the Hebrew language as a design for a t-shirt. Hebrew is the language of Judaism.

In Judaism the word **ahava** is translated as love. It literally means 'I give'. For Jews, love means giving and expecting nothing in return. Jews are commanded to:
- love God with all your heart, with all your soul and with all your strength; and
- love your neighbour as yourself.

The Mishnah, an important Jewish text, describes ahava as:

… good deeds, willingness to sacrifice your life rather than commit certain serious sins, willingness to sacrifice all of your possessions, and being grateful to the Lord despite difficulties.

Knowledge check

1. Who or what is Allah?
2. Whom should Muslims love above all others?
3. What is the literal meaning of ahava?
4. Where are Jews commanded to direct their love?

Activity A

Compose an acrostic poem about love using the letters of the words metta, ahava and agape to start each line. Use the descriptions of these words to help you.

Sikhism

Sikhs believe that love comes from God. A person who shows their love and compassion for others will receive God's blessing.

You have no compassion; the Lord's Light does not shine in you.
You are drowned, drowned in worldly entanglements.

(from the Guru Granth Sahib)

Activity B

1. Make a poster showing religious ideas about love.
2. Look through some newspapers and magazines to find articles and pictures that show examples of religious ideas about love in action.

Activity C

Find more quotations about and definitions of love from the religions mentioned in this chapter. Are there any differences between them? Make a poster highlighting any differences you find.

Activity D

Complete Activity C. Is it possible to come up with a definition of love that all religions would agree with? Have a go! Afterwards, think about how successful you have been.

3.7 What is justice?

Learning objectives

You will …
- learn about the lives of Elizabeth Fry and Bhimrao Ambedkar
- understand the connection between love and justice.

Justice is about being fair to people while respecting their rights as human beings. For religious people, it is a way to put the love they feel for others into practice.

Bhimrao Ambedkar

Dr Ambedkar on an Indian stamp.

Bhimrao Ramji Ambedkar was born in India in 1891. He belonged to a class of people called Untouchables. Untouchables were social outcasts: they could not get a good education or employment.

Ambedkar struggled to get a good education. His father managed to get him a place in a school, but he was not allowed to sit with other children, and was not even allowed to drink water from a cup in case he contaminated it.

Ambedkar studied hard and got into university. He became highly qualified, gaining a doctorate in law in London.

He became a Buddhist, and devoted his life to the fight against the system that labelled some people 'untouchable'. As a politician, he drafted the Indian constitution which gave rights of freedom for all groups of people, and finally made untouchability unlawful.

Siddhartha Gautama, the Buddha, said:

If beings knew, as I know, the results of sharing gifts, they would not enjoy their gifts without sharing them with others.

(Itivuttaka Sutta 18)

He also said:

However many holy words you read, however many you speak, what good will they do you if you do not act on upon them?

(Dhammapada)

Elizabeth Fry

Elizabeth Fry features on the British five-pound note.

In the Christian Bible, St Paul writes:

Remember those in prison as if you were their fellow prisoners, and those who are maltreated as if you yourselves were suffering.

(Hebrews 13:3)

St James writes:

Faith without action is dead.

(James 2:17)

Elizabeth Fry was born into a Christian family in 1780. She had a very keen sense of love for others and wanted to help them. She visited prisoners in Newgate Gaol (prison) in London and was horrified at the conditions they lived in, particularly the women and their children.

She provided them with clothes and food. She started a school for the children, and got work for the prisoners. She persuaded the government to change prison conditions for the better. She went on to help the poor and homeless, and even started a training school for nurses.

Knowledge check

Out of Bhimrao Ambedkar and Elizabeth Fry, who:
- was born in India?
- was a Buddhist?
- taught children in prison?
- was an Untouchable?
- was a Christian?
- made the government change conditions for poorer social groups?

The chocolate connection

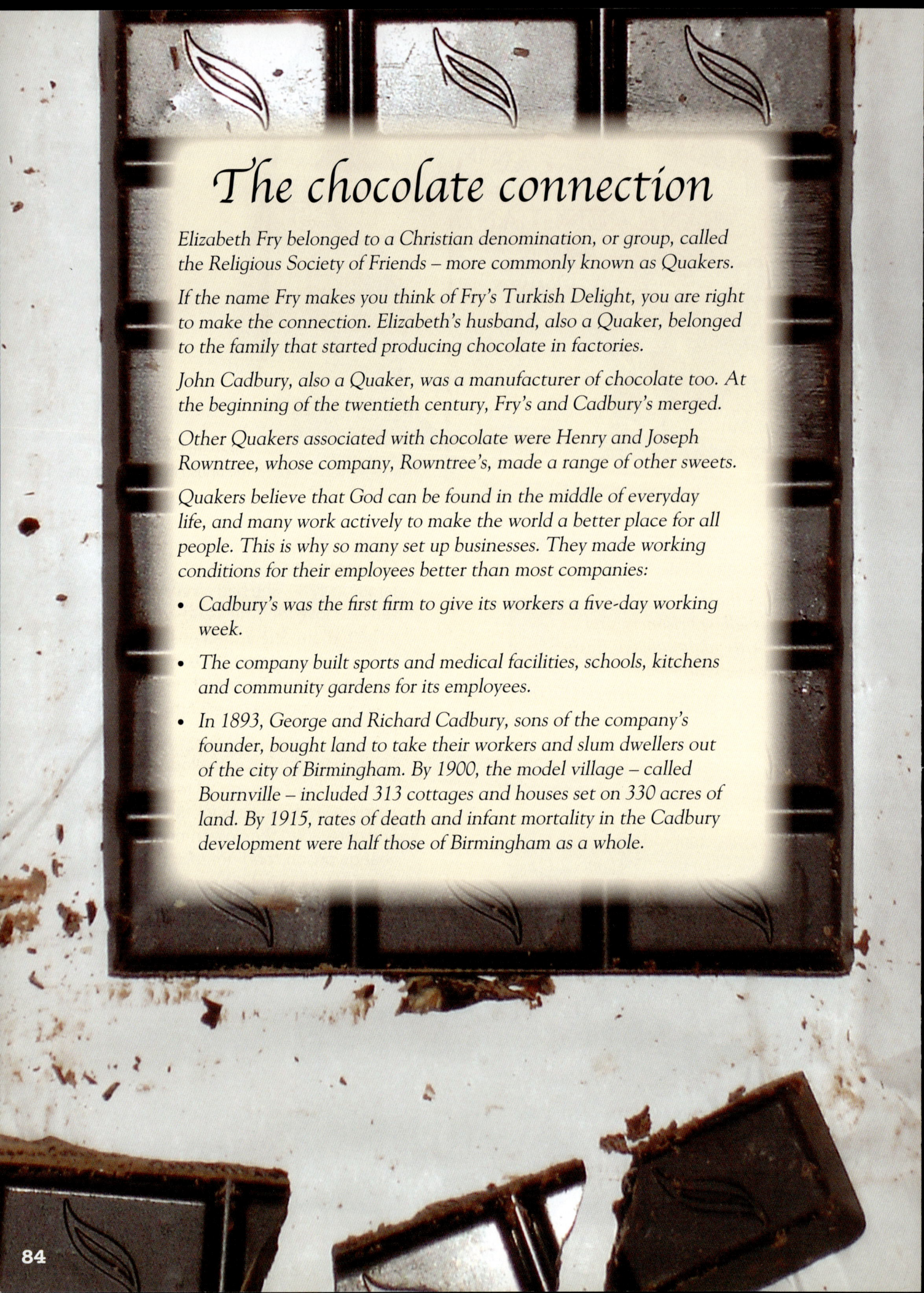

Elizabeth Fry belonged to a Christian denomination, or group, called the Religious Society of Friends – more commonly known as Quakers.

If the name Fry makes you think of Fry's Turkish Delight, you are right to make the connection. Elizabeth's husband, also a Quaker, belonged to the family that started producing chocolate in factories.

John Cadbury, also a Quaker, was a manufacturer of chocolate too. At the beginning of the twentieth century, Fry's and Cadbury's merged.

Other Quakers associated with chocolate were Henry and Joseph Rowntree, whose company, Rowntree's, made a range of other sweets.

Quakers believe that God can be found in the middle of everyday life, and many work actively to make the world a better place for all people. This is why so many set up businesses. They made working conditions for their employees better than most companies:

- Cadbury's was the first firm to give its workers a five-day working week.
- The company built sports and medical facilities, schools, kitchens and community gardens for its employees.
- In 1893, George and Richard Cadbury, sons of the company's founder, bought land to take their workers and slum dwellers out of the city of Birmingham. By 1900, the model village – called Bournville – included 313 cottages and houses set on 330 acres of land. By 1915, rates of death and infant mortality in the Cadbury development were half those of Birmingham as a whole.

Servants of society

> I have seen Elizabeth Fry in Newgate and I have witnessed the miraculous effects of true Christianity upon the most depraved of human beings.

John Randolph, American Envoy to England (February, 1819).

Bhimrao Ambedkar.

> A great man is (someone who) ... is ready to be the servant of society.

Activity A

Find out more about the life of Elizabeth Fry. Make a poster using words and images to illustrate it.

Activity B

1 Find out more about the life of Dr Ambedkar. You could present important events in his life in the form of a storyboard.
2 Dr Ambedkar was born into a Hindu family and became a Buddhist later in life. Find out why he made this change.
3 What did he find unsatisfactory in Hinduism, and why did he find Buddhism more satisfactory? Include this in your storyboard.

Activity C

Read Dr Ambedkar's quote above about being a servant of society.
1 What do you think Dr Ambedkar meant by this?
2 Give examples from his life and the life of Elizabeth Fry.

Activity D

Justice is love in action.
1 How far do you agree with this statement?
2 Use the religious definitions of love that you investigated in the last chapter, and examples of ways in which religious people have worked to make the lives of others better.

3.8 Why is forgiveness important?

Learning objectives

You will …
- learn what forgiveness means for religious people
- understand why religions teach that people should forgive those who do them wrong
- interpret some religious teachings about forgiveness.

The Return of the Prodigal Son by Rembrandt is based on a famous Bible story about forgiveness. Which emotions is the painter able to show in this picture?

Activity A

1. Read the Buddhism 2 quotation on page 87.
2. Write a short story to show what it means.

Activity B

1. Read through all the quotations on page 87.
2. Give as many reasons as you can why the religions teach that people should forgive those who do them wrong.

Christianity 1
And when you stand praying, if you hold a grudge against anyone, forgive him, so that your Father in heaven may forgive you your sins.

Islam
Although a fair punishment for an offence is to repay in kind, those who forgive … are rewarded by Allah. He does not love the unjust.

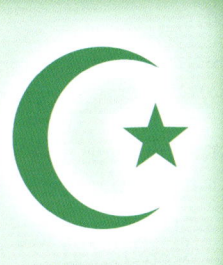

Christianity 2
Do not judge, and you will not be judged. Do not condemn, and you will not be condemned. Forgive, and you will be forgiven.

Buddhism 2
Holding on to anger is like grasping a hot coal with the intent of throwing it at someone else; you are the one who gets burnt.

Hinduism
There is only one problem with forgiving: people think a forgiving person is weak. That is a mistake, however, for forgiveness is a great power. Forgiveness is a virtue of the weak, and an ornament of the strong. Forgiveness can overpower anything; what is there that forgiveness cannot achieve? What can a wicked person do to a person who carries the sword of forgiveness in his hand? Fire falling on grassless ground is extinguished of itself. An unforgiving individual disgraces himself terribly.

Buddhism 1
Hatred does not stop in this world by hating, but by not hating; this is an eternal truth.

Sikhism
Where there is falsehood, there is sin.
Where there is greed, there is death.
Where there is forgiveness, God Himself is there.

Activity C
1. Read the quotation from Hinduism.
2. Do you agree that it is a mistake to think that it is weak to forgive and that forgiveness is a power?
3. In your answer, try to give some examples from your own life or that of someone you know.

Activity D
An American thinker called Reinhold Niebuhr said, *'Forgiveness is the final form of love.'*
1. What do you think he meant by this?
2. Do you agree with him? Give reasons or examples to support your answer.

To forgive or not?

Nepal blast victims forgive the bombers

by Chirendra Satyal, Kathmandu

People who have lost loved ones or who were injured by a bomb blast that rocked Kathmandu's Assumption Church last year say they have forgiven the people who carried out the attack.

'I have gone and met the two main people responsible for killing my wife and daughter,' said parishioner Balan Joseph. 'I have forgiven them and am praying for them.'

Joseph was speaking at a ceremony on May 23, Pentecost Sunday, which also commemorated the tragedy that took place exactly a year ago. The blast killed three people and injured several others.

The recent ceremony, which included prayers and hymns for Nepal, was held in an open field near Assumption Church. Hundreds of Christians, including pastors of various Christian Churches, attended the event.

Other victims of the tragedy told UCA News they had forgiven those responsible for their pain.

'I have forgiven them completely. I feel that even difficulties are part of God's plan for me,' said Samuel Rai, who spent four months in hospital recovering from severe burns.

Union of Catholic Asian News, 24 May 2010

> Everyone says forgiveness is a lovely idea, until they have something to forgive.

C. S. Lewis

Activity A

1. Re-read the articles on pages 88–89. What reason does Samuel Rai (above) give for forgiving the killers in Kathmandu?

2. What reasons does Julie Nicholson (page 89) give for not forgiving the killers of her daughter?

Activity B

Do you agree that Julie Nicholson (page 89) should not remain as a vicar in the Church because she cannot forgive her daughter's killers? Give reasons for your answer.

Vicar grappling with grief stands down over bombers who took her daughter's life

Even the Reverend Julie Nicholson's Christian faith has not helped her to forgive the suicide bombers who took her daughter's life. Perhaps that would be too much to expect of any mother.

Exactly eight months since the London bombings on 7 July last year, Mrs Nicholson has given up her job as an inner-city vicar because she feels unable to preach a message of peace and reconciliation when she does not feel it in her heart.

Jennifer Nicholson, her talented, vivacious, 24-year-old daughter, was one of 56 people who died in the bombings. Her mother, vicar of the parish of St Aidan with St George in Bristol, has suffered the double bereavement of losing not just her daughter but also the vocation that she loved. Mrs Nicholson said: 'It's very difficult for me to stand behind an altar and celebrate the Eucharist, the Communion, and lead people in words of peace and reconciliation and forgiveness when I feel very far from that myself. So, for the time being, that wound in me is having to heal.'

Mrs Nicholson says that not only could she not forgive the killers, she does not want to forgive. She said: 'I will leave potential forgiveness for whatever is after this life. I will leave that in God's hands.'

Every day she says the name of Mohammad Sidique Khan (one of the four bombers). 'I have a certain amount of pity for the fact that four young people felt that this was something they had to do but I certainly don't have any sense of compassion. Can I forgive them for what they did? No, I cannot.

'I believe that there are some things in life which are unforgivable by the human spirit. We are all faced with choice and those four human beings on that day chose to do what they did.'

The Times, 7 March 2006

Activity C

What might a Christian say to try to persuade Julie Nicholson to try to forgive, and how might she answer? Write out your response in the form of a dialogue.

Activity D

Holding on to your resentment means you are locked into your victimhood – and you allow the perpetrator to have a hold over your life. When you forgive, you let go, it sets you free, and it will probably set free the perpetrator. There is much to be won from making yourself a little vulnerable.

(Archbishop Desmond Tutu)

1. What does Archbishop Tutu mean when he says, 'Holding on to your resentment means you are locked into your victimhood'?
2. Do you agree with him? Give reasons for your answer.
3. Why might some people disagree with you?

The big assignment

Task
To create a behaviour policy for your school based on the Golden Rule.

Objectives
- To turn the Golden Rule into guidelines for behaviour in your school.
- To promote your behaviour policy in your school.
- To present your behaviour policy to the governors of your school.

Outcome
To produce a set of resources to promote your behaviour policy.

Guidance

1. Work in groups of four or five. Decide what needs to be done and who is going to do it.

2. Your group should aim to produce the following:
   - a list of rules for conduct in the classroom, with at least one reason for each
   - a list of rules for conduct outside the classroom, with at least one reason for each
   - posters of the Golden Rule to remind people what the rules are based on
   - posters of the classroom rules for various teaching areas
   - a PowerPoint® presentation for a school assembly on 'Consequences: the rewards and sanctions (punishments) for upholding or breaking the policy'.

3. Your group will need to think about:
   - how people should be expected to behave towards each other
   - how people should be expected to treat other people's property
   - what should happen to people who break the rules (punishments)
   - what should happen to people who consistently support the rules (rewards)
   - how people can feel they have been treated fairly
   - the part pupils can play in managing the system.

4. You will need to revise the following ideas:
   - the Golden Rule
   - rules about right and wrong
   - love – respect, kindness, trust
   - justice
   - forgiveness.

5. When you have completed the tasks, try to arrange a meeting with some of the governors of your school to present your ideas to them.

Assessment

You will be assessed on:
- ✓ your understanding of the Golden Rule
- ✓ how you make rules based on the Golden Rule
- ✓ your understanding of justice.

Glossary

agape love, putting the welfare of other people before your own (Christianity)

ahava love, given to people by God to be given to others (Judaism)

ahimsa avoiding harming or using violence against living beings (Buddhism, Hinduism)

Allah the one God (Islam)

ark a cupboard at the front of a synagogue where holy scrolls are kept (Judaism)

aureole a circle of light surrounding the head or body of a holy being in some religious art

avatar a god in human form (Hinduism)

Big Bang an explosion thought to have marked the beginning of the universe

Big Crunch the idea that the universe may stop expanding and collapse on itself

Big Freeze the idea that the universe may get too cold for anything to live

Big Rip the idea that the universe may expand so fast that it will rip apart

Brahma the creator God (Hinduism)

Buddha an enlightened being; also used to refer to the first Buddha in recorded history, Siddhartha Gautama (Buddhism)

conscience an awareness of what is right and wrong

convert a person who has changed their religious faith or other belief

crucifix a cross with a figure of Jesus on it

devas a god (Hinduism)

divinity a god

doctrine a religious teaching

dualism the view that a human being consists of a body and a separate mind

dukkha suffering (Buddhism)

enlightened being a person who has found the way to overcome suffering and achieve perfect happiness (Buddhism)

eschatology religious beliefs and teachings about the end of time

Five Precepts guidelines for behaviour (Buddhism)

Ganesha A popular Hindu god

Golden Rule A code that requires people to treat others as they would like to be treated

gurdwara a place of worship (Sikhism)

Guru Nanak the person who inspired the Sikh faith

identity the set of characteristics that make up a person's individuality

also see **personal identity**

also see **social identity**

karma the idea that a person's actions affect what will happen to them in the future

lectern a stand to support a holy book when it is read in public

Messiah a king, expected by the Jews to lead people back to God (Christians believe that Jesus was the Messiah)

metta loving-kindness (Buddhism)

mezuzah a scroll of biblical text in a case attached to a doorframe (Judaism)

mihrab a niche in the wall of a mosque to indicate the direction of Makkah (Islam)

minbar a small staircase from which the sermon is delivered in a mosque (Islam)

missionary a person who spreads their faith to others

moral dilemma a situation in which a person must choose between two unsatisfactory alternatives

mosque a Muslim place of worship (Islam)

persecute to continue to treat an individual or group of people unfairly

personal identity individuality

philosopher a person who thinks about and tries to explain ideas about life

physicalism the view that a person is entirely physical or material

prophet a person who believes he or she has a message from God

psychologist a person who studies human behaviour

Ramayana a long poem about the adventures of Rama (Hinduism)

revelation the revealing of God's will to a human being

sadhu a wandering holy man (Hinduism)

science the study of the physical world

seven dimensions seven features of a religion or worldview

Shabbat the Jewish day of rest and worship, celebrated on Saturday (Judaism)

Shiva the god of destruction (Hinduism)

shrine an area reserved for worship

social identity aspects of an individual's personal identity that are influenced by the groups they belong to

submission the giving up of one's own will to that of another

symbol a sign or character that represents a complex idea

synagogue a Jewish place of worship (Judaism)

Ten Commandments Laws believed to have been given by God. They summarise how humans should act towards God and each other

Trinity God seen in three ways: Father, Son (Jesus Christ) and Holy Spirit (Christianity)

Trimurti the Hindu Gods of creation, preservation and destruction: Brahma, Vishnu and Shiva (Hinduism)

Vishnu the preserver God (Hinduism)

Worldview a common framework of ideas about life shared by a group of people

Index

Abraham 9, 42
Adam and Eve 44, 47
Ambedkar, Bhimrao 82, 83, 85
The Ancient of Days 49
art, religious symbols in 16–19

beliefs 36–7, 38, 47
   in God 37, 40–3
   and human life 44–7
the Bible (Christian) 15, 49, 51
   on justice 83
the Big Bang 48, 49
the Big Crunch 52
the Big Freeze 52
the Big Rip 52
bombings
   Kathmandu 88
   London 89
Bournville 84
Brahma/Brahman 45, 53, 54
Brick Lane Mosque (London) 23
the Buddha (Siddhartha Gautama) 9, 16, 28
   on justice 82
   statues of 68
Buddhism
   beliefs 43, 45, 46, 47
   and conscience 59
   development of 28, 29
   and forgiveness 87
   the Golden Rule 66
   guiding principles of 62, 64
   and Jesus 15
   and justice 82, 85
   metta 78
   and moral dilemmas 76
   shrines 25
   symbols of in art 16
   teachers 11
   temples 21
   The Wheel of Life 46

Cadbury family 84
Christianity 8, 28, 29, 65
   beliefs 42, 43, 44, 47
   churches 21, 22, 23
   and conscience 59
   converts to 27
   crucifixes 26
   Day of Judgement 55
   and forgiveness 86, 87, 88, 89
   the Golden Rule 66

   and Jesus 12, 42, 54
   and love (agape) 79
   and moral dilemmas 76
   symbols of in art 17, 18
   Stations of the Cross 21
   the Trinity 6, 17, 42
   and the universe 49
conscience 58–61
creationism 51
crucifixes 26

Day of Judgement 54, 55
Descartes, René 32
development of religions 27–9
doctrine 28
dualism 32, 33

eschatology 53

faith 36–7
forgiveness 86–9, 91
Fry, Elizabeth 83, 84, 85

Ganesha 18
God 6, 9, 37, 40–3
the Golden Rule 66–9, 76, 90, 91
Golden Temple (Harmandir Sahib) 68, 69
guiding principles of religions 62–5
Guru Nanak 8, 19

Hinduism 9, 12, 62
   ahimsa 62, 63, 79
   beliefs 43, 45, 46, 47
   and conscience 59
   and forgiveness 87
   the Golden Rule 66
   offerings 21
   the Ramayana 25
   symbols of in art 18
   temples 21
   the Trimurti 53, 54
   and the universe 50, 53
homes of religious families 24–6
human beings 32–5
   religious beliefs about 44–7

icons 18
identity 34–5
incense 21

Islam 8, 28, 29, 64
    Allah 13, 42, 80
    beliefs 42, 43, 44, 47
    and conscience 59
    Day of Judgement 54
    and forgiveness 87
    the Golden Rule 66
    Jesus in 13, 15
    mosques 20, 22, 23
    the Qur'an 13, 15, 25, 51, 80

Jerusalem 27
Jesus 8, 14–15, 42, 54
    non-Christian religions and 12–15
    representations of 7, 17
Judaism 9, 27, 29, 62
    ahava 80
    the ark 20
    beliefs 42, 43, 44, 47
    the Golden Rule 66
    the Messiah 54
    mezuzahs 24
    and moral dilemmas 76
    and the Roman Empire 27
    Shabbat 26
    synagogues 20, 23
    and the universe 49
justice 82–5, 91

karma 18, 45, 47, 79

lecterns 22
Les Miserables (Hugo) 73
love 78–81, 85, 87, 91

Mary, mother of Jesus 17
moral dilemmas 70–7
    examples of 70–3
    solving 74–7
Muhammad 8, 42
music in places of worship 22

Nicholson, Julie 89

origins of religions 8–9
Orthodox Church 18, 28

personal identity 34–5
physicalism 33
the Pope 28
prophets 42

Quakers (Religious Society of Friends) 84
Qur'an 25, 51, 80
    and Isa (Jesus) 13, 15

religion, origins of the word 34
Roman Catholic Church 18, 28
Rowntree, Henry and Joseph 84

science and the universe 48, 51, 52, 55
seven dimensions of religion 38–9
Shabbat 26
Shichiri Kojun 11
Shiva 53, 54
shrines 25
Sikhism 8, 62, 64, 81
    beliefs 43, 45, 46, 47
    and forgiveness 87
    the Golden Rule 66
    the Golden Temple 68, 69
    gurdwaras 21, 22
    symbols of in art 19
social identity 34–5
symbols 4–7
    of identity 35
    religious 5–7, 45
        in art 16–19
synagogues 20, 23

Taoism 67
teachers 10–11
temples 21
the Trinity 6, 17, 42
Tutu, Archbishop Desmond 89

the universe 48–55
    future of 52–5
    origins of 48–51

violence 65
Vishnu 53, 54

worldviews 39
worship, places of 20–3, 30–1

Zoroastrianism 66

The Publishers would like to thank the following for permission to reproduce copyright material:

Photo credits
p.5 *tl* © The Granger Collection, NYC/TopFoto, *tr* © Jason Stitt – Fotolia, *bl* © Yuri Arcurs – Fotolia, *br* © Duncan Noakes – Fotolia; **p.13** © The Art Archive/Alamy; **p.14** *t* © Art Directors & TRIP/Alamy, *bl* © dreamtours/SuperStock, *br* © Friedrich Stark/Alamy; **p.16** © Fraser Hall/SuperStock; **p.17** *t* © akg-images, *b* © The Print Collector /Alamy; **p.18** © photosindia/Getty Images; **p.19** © age fotostock/SuperStock; **p.20** *l* © Godong/SuperStock, *r* © mlehmann78 – Fotolia; **p.21** *tl* © AP/Press Association Images, *tr* © Greenshoots Communications/Alamy, *bl* © Simon Au, *br* © Ronnie – Fotolia; **p.22** *tl* © DEA/C. SAPPA/Getty Images, *tr* © Andres Rodriguez – Fotolia, *b* © Art Directors & TRIP/Alamy; **p.23** © So-Shan Au; **p.24** © Shaffer/Smith/SuperStock; **p.25** *t* © Stories of the Prophets in the Holy Qur'an, Author: Ruth Woodhall, Illustrations: Shahada (Sharelle) Abdul Haqq, Publisher: Tugrah Books, New Jersey, USA, 2008, *c* © Louise Batalla Duran/Alamy, *b* © Alen MacWeeney/Corbis; **pp.30–31** © Dusart/Sunset/Rex Features; **p.32** © Bettmann/Corbis; **p.48** © NASA; **p.49** © 2010 SuperStock; **p.53** © Art Directors & TRIP/Alamy; **p.55** © Image Asset Management Ltd/SuperStock; **p.69** © Natalia Lysenko – Fotolia; **p.78** © Jordan Lewy – Fotolia; **p.79** © Agape Unlimited, Inc.; **p.80** Hebrew Love Tattoo © RJ Roth, Rotem Gear, RotemGear.com. Reprinted with permission; **p.82** © Hipix/ Alamy; **p.83** © NILS JORGENSEN/Rex Features; **p.84** © Stephen Preston; **p.86** © Bridgeman Art Library, London/SuperStock; **p.90–91** © Peter Cade/Getty Images.

Acknowledgements
p.40 'I believe there is a God' screenshot © Artem Karimov/http://commons.wikimedia.org/wiki/File:Europe_belief_in_god.svg#File_history/Creative Commons http://creativecommons.org/licenses/by-sa/3.0/deed.en; **p.41** bar chart showing spiritual beliefs for the EU and UK, adapted from Special Eurobarometer 225: Social Values, Science & Technology; **p.51** Creationism article adapted from an article in the *Education Guardian*, 5 October 2007; **p.88** article from the *Union of Catholic Asian News*, 24 May 2010; **p.89** article from *The Times*, 7 March 2006, © Simon de Bruxelles/*The Times*/nisyndication.

Every effort has been made to trace all copyright holders, but if any have been inadvertently overlooked the Publishers will be pleased to make the necessary arrangements at the first opportunity.